Deliverance

The Principles and Practice of Deliverance Ministry

PATTY KATZER & MALCOLM WEBBER

Published by:

Strategic Press
www.StrategicPress.org

Strategic Press is a division of Strategic Global Assistance, Inc.
www.sgai.org

513 S. Main St. Suite 2
Elkhart, IN 46516
U.S.A.

+1-844-532-3371 (LEADER-1)

Copyright © 2000 Malcolm Webber & Patty Katzer

ISBN: 978-1-888810-21-9

All Scripture references are from the New International Version of the Bible, unless otherwise noted.

Printed in the United States of America

Contents

Introduction 7
Chapter 1: The Scriptures: Our Source of Knowledge 9
Chapter 2: The Greatness of God 19
Chapter 3: The Origin and Nature of Satan 23
Chapter 4: The Origin and Nature of Demons 41
Chapter 5: The Christian and Deliverance 57
Chapter 6: Preparation for Deliverance 73
Chapter 7: Setting Yourself Free 91
Chapter 8: Praying for Others to Be Set Free 99
Chapter 9: Conclusion 109
Selected Bibliography 111

Introduction

In Scripture, the term "deliverance" is often used interchangeably with the term "salvation." It is an all-encompassing concept describing the redemptive work of God as it relates to man. In this study, the term will be used in its technical application as it relates to deliverance from evil spirits by the power of God (e.g., Matt. 12:28). Thus, deliverance can be defined as the expulsion of a demon (or demons) from a human by the power of the Holy Spirit through faith in Jesus Christ.

Deliverance can occur in many ways. At times simply hearing the Word of God with a heart to obey will initiate deliverance. An act of forgiveness may be enough to drive out a demon without further warfare. Life-changing events such as the experience of salvation, baptism in water, or the baptism in the Holy Spirit may precipitate the exit of demon powers in a person's life. Sometimes simply resisting is sufficient. However, in many cases, demons are strongly entrenched, and a more focused and deliberate deliverance initiative is required for a believer to realize the freedom from bondage that Jesus provided by His death and resurrection. Jesus empowered and commanded His followers to deal with demons by casting them out. The Greek word *ekballo*, translated "cast out" means to eject, cast forth, thrust out, drive out, or expel.

About one third of the public ministry of Jesus Christ involved casting out demons. This is because demonic activity is encountered everywhere. While the Bible does not major on the presence and activity of Satan and his helpers, it clearly presents them as real enemies of God and man, describing their nature and function in many passages.

The casting out of demons is an inseparable part of the commission Jesus gave to His church (Mark 16:16-17). Thus, the ministry of deliverance is an integral part of the work of the ministry (Eph. 4:16) that all believers should be trained in, both for their own benefit and as part of their equipping to minister to others.

This brief guide is intended to provide scriptural and practical information to equip the believer to launch out in this life-changing aspect of ministry as it relates to himself and others.

Patricia Katzer & Malcolm Webber, Ph.D.
2001

The Scriptures: Our Source of Knowledge

A great variety of opinions is held throughout the church today concerning Satan and the powers of darkness. The most prevalent examples are:

1. Satan does not exist. According to this view, Satan is merely the personification of evil. In addressing Satan as a personality, Jesus was catering to the ignorance of the ancient people in their superstitious beliefs. Most people who hold this view would also deny the deity of Christ and the authority of Scriptures.
2. Satan exists, but only in places like Africa and India. "We've heard the missionaries' wild stories, but it couldn't happen in the 'civilized world'!" Proponents of this view do not see any correlation between bowing to a wooden image and bowing to the god of materialism.
3. Satan exists, but he is nothing to be concerned about, since Jesus defeated him at the cross. This view is overly simplistic and ignores the obvious fact that Satan and his evil forces are oppressing multitudes of Christians as well as non-Christians. Those holding this view would object to the study of Satan and deliverance, believing it to "glorify Satan."
4. Satan exists, and he is everywhere and behind everything! Those who hold this view are paralyzed by their preoccu-

pation with Satan and his activity. They not only believe in deliverance, but they make it the centerpiece of Christian experience. As one writer improperly described the Christian life: "deliverance is the engine and the train."
5. Satan is a real, personal, finite being who opposes God, His purposes, and His people. This is the biblical view.

Each of the first four views falls short of the scriptural balance and will thereby serve the purpose of Satan. Our understanding of our adversary will determine how we respond or fail to respond to him and his works of destruction. If we ignore him, he is free to move about unhindered, yet an over-emphasis on the enemy will turn our attention from God and His purposes. The biblical balance is to focus on God, but also to understand our adversary for the purpose of recognizing his activity and engaging in spiritual warfare to defeat him.

THE BALANCE

If we're going to win a battle we must know our enemy – not as well as we know God, of course, but we must not be ignorant. Our purpose is not to glorify Satan, but to expose him. Every time he's exposed, his position is weakened.

We must know our enemy and be good at dealing with him, but we must also stay balanced – for our own sake and for the sake of the people to whom we minister. A number of ministries over the years over-emphasized the ministry of deliverance and many were hurt in the end. They became lopsided and lost focus. Some lost reality.

Jesus spent only about a third of His public ministry dealing with demons. Furthermore, in His private ministry He dealt very little with the devil. He concentrated on His time with His disciples: mentoring and developing them, and raising them up as leaders. Then, in His private life, Jesus spent much time with His Father. Jesus spent considerably more time with His Father than He did involved with the devil.

The Christian life is about the Lord Jesus.

> *Now this is eternal life: that they may know you, the only true God, and Jesus Christ, whom you have sent. (John 17:3)*

It is not about the devil. Fellowship with God must be the foundation of our lives and ministries, not involvement with Satan. We need to be obsessed with God, not with Satan. We must be fascinated with God, not preoccupied with the enemy.

On the other hand, we do have a great need for knowledge concerning demons:

> *lest Satan should take advantage of us; for we are not ignorant of his devices. (2 Cor. 2:11, NKJV)*

According to Paul, if we are ignorant of Satan and his "devices," he will be able to "take advantage" of us.

Therefore, while our ministries should not "specialize" in demons, we must be equipped to deal with them. Part of our calling as Christians involves dealing directly with the powers of darkness. We are commanded in Scripture to:

- Cast out demon spirits (Matt. 10:7-8; Mark 16:17).
- Pull down strongholds (2 Cor. 10:3-4).
- Not give the devil a "foothold" (Eph. 4:27).
- Be good soldiers and wage a good warfare (1 Tim. 1:18; 6:12).
- Resist the devil (Jam. 4:7; 1 Pet. 5:8-9). We are not to ignore Satan, but resist him.

We are in a war fighting against a highly organized and powerful foe. Yet, large portions of the church in the Western world aren't sure if the enemy even truly exists! Moreover, many churches who do believe in Satan have no significant knowledge of his ways or how to deal with him.

Could you imagine one nation going into battle with another nation and doing so with no understanding of the enemy or its weapons or tactics? Even worse, could you imagine a nation going into a war without training its own troops? Of course, that is foolishness. We would not conceive of one nation fighting another without as much knowledge as it can get and without as much training and discipline of its troops as possible. Yet, the church does just this.

Some churches are quite knowledgeable about the enemy, but even then they are not always where they should be – in the battle.

As representatives of the kingdom of God, we should be fighting against spiritual darkness for our families, our churches, our cities, and whatever regions that God has placed before us.

If you're not in the battle you're probably living a defeated life. Many Christians are living in defeat, many marriages and families are in confusion, and many churches are defeated, when victory lies within our grasp. It's not that hard!

However, just as a nation would not go into battle without extensive training of its troops and gaining information of the enemy's position, tactics, and weaponry, so the church cannot be successful without knowledge of its adversary, and training in how to overcome him.

We must know:

- Our God – who He is and what He has commanded us to do.
- Ourselves – our position and authority in Christ, our weapons and tactics.
- Our enemy – who he is, his weapons and tactics.

Then God commands us to fight:

> *Finally, be strong in the Lord and in his mighty power. Put on the full armor of God so that you can take your stand against the devil's*

> *schemes. For our struggle is not against flesh and blood, but against the rulers, against the authorities, against the powers of this dark world and against the spiritual forces of evil in the heavenly realms. Therefore put on the full armor of God, so that when the day of evil comes, you may be able to stand your ground, and after you have done everything, to stand. (Eph. 6:10-13)*

If we do this, we will win. If we fight, we will win. We may lose a battle or two on the way, but we will win the war. The outcome is as certain as God's Word!

So, in order to be effective Christians, and in order to fulfill our purposes on this earth and in the church, we must be knowledgeable about Satan and about his devices (his ways and means).

THE WORD OF GOD IS OUR SOURCE OF INFORMATION

In our quest to gain knowledge of Satan and his tactics, we must avoid seeking information from questionable sources. Many sources of information today offer explanations for the presence of evil. Even Hollywood has undertaken to portray the spiritual side of reality through modern occult films. However, only one source of information is reliable.

> *All Scripture is God-breathed and is useful for teaching, rebuking, correcting and training in righteousness, so that the man of God may be thoroughly equipped for every good work. (2 Tim. 3:16-17)*

We must receive our knowledge of Satan from the Word of God. Some people have tried to gain knowledge of the spiritual realm by conversing with demons during deliverance sessions. The folly of this is exposed in the classic dialogue:

> Deliverance minister: "Demon, what is your name?"
> Demon: "I'm a lying spirit!"
> Deliverance minister: "You lying spirit, are you telling me the truth?"

Of course, this kind of conversation will not get you very far! If the demon says it is a lying spirit, how would you know it's telling the truth? If the demon says it is not a lying spirit, how could you know it's telling the truth, because it may just be lying about it. Thus, it would be an endless circle – because demons lie. It is the nature of demons to lie, so anything they say is suspect. Jesus declared concerning Satan:

> ...*he is a liar and the father of lies. (John 8:44)*

In His ministry, Jesus spoke to demons only occasionally, and then He did so very briefly and with a clear purpose.

To hold extended conversations with demons is foolish and an open door for deception.

WE MUST NOT GO BEYOND THE WORD OF GOD

There is much about the spiritual realm that is hidden from us. Moreover, God intends it to be that way – or else He would have revealed it to us in His Word.

Therefore, we must not go beyond the Word of God. The written Word of God is sufficient. In fact, there is more than enough in the Word of God for the greatest and most brilliant men and women to spend a lifetime learning and obeying, without looking beyond it for some deeper truth or hidden key. How tragic that countless lives have been shipwrecked over the centuries as people departed from the clearly revealed Word of God and ventured into areas they should not have. Let us have the heart of King David:

> *My heart is not proud, O Lord, my eyes are not haughty; I do not concern myself with great matters or things too wonderful for me. (Psalm 131:1)*

David, who was called a man after God's own heart, knew his own limits. He was content to let some matters remain in God's domain.

The Bible, while entirely true and absolutely authoritative, is also selective (e.g., John 20:30-31; 21:25). God's purpose in giving us the Scripture was not to answer every question that our minds could possibly conceive, but to reveal what we need to believe and obey Him. Much about the spiritual realm is hidden from us by God's own design.

> *The secret things belong to the* Lord *our God, but the things revealed belong to us and to our children forever, that we may follow all the words of this law. (Deut. 29:29)*

From the history of creation to the final triumph of the Son of God, the Scriptures, through precept and example, contain all we need to know about Satan and the spiritual realm.

WE MUST NOT BE ARROGANT IN DEALING WITH SATAN

It is common today to hear ministers refer to Satan in derogatory terms or even make fun of him. Jesus, who is our model, never did this. We are not to honor the devil, but neither are we to revile him.

Peter, the apostle, soundly condemns such arrogant disrespect.

> *and especially those who walk according to the flesh in the lust of uncleanness and despise authority. They are presumptuous, self-willed. They are not afraid to speak evil of dignitaries, whereas angels, who are greater in power and might, do not bring a reviling accusation against them before the Lord. But these, like natural brute beasts made to be caught and destroyed, speak evil of the things they do not understand, and will utterly perish in their own corruption, (2 Pet. 2:10-12, NKJV; cf. Jude 8-10)*

> *Be sober, be vigilant; because your adversary the devil walks about like a roaring lion, seeking whom he may devour. Resist him, steadfast in the faith, knowing that the same sufferings are experienced by your brotherhood in the world. (1 Pet. 5:8-9, NKJV)*

Our resistance to Satan is in the context of sobriety, not foolishness, flippancy or carelessness. Satan is powerful. He is like a roaring lion. He has deceived and destroyed billions of men, women, and children, many of whom were very gifted and intelligent. Insulting names have no place in our warfare.

STUDY QUESTIONS

1. Explain why we must know about Satan and demons.
2. What advantage does Satan have when churches ignore him?
3. What advantage does Satan have when churches overemphasize him?
4. What influences other than the Bible have shaped your understanding of God, Satan, and the spiritual realm?

The Greatness of God

No work on the topic of deliverance should be approached without first emphasizing the greatness of God. As previously stated, our focus in deliverance, as well as every other area of life and ministry, is on God, not Satan or demons. God, eternally manifested as Father, Son, and Holy Spirit, is uncreated, eternal Spirit, whose power and wisdom are without limit and beyond all comprehension. In addition to His transcendent perfections such as omnipotence, omniscience, and omnipresence, He possesses flawless moral attributes such as righteousness, holiness, love, and justice. Meditating upon these virtues of God will stir our hearts to worship and joyful obedience (cf. Ps. 95) and will give us the scriptural perspective in our dealings with the forces of darkness.

> *You alone are the Lord. You made the heavens, even the highest heavens, and all their starry host, the earth and all that is on it, the seas and all that is in them. You give life to everything, and the multitudes of heaven worship you. (Neh. 9:6)*

> *The Lord has established his throne in heaven, and his kingdom rules over all. (Ps. 103:19)*

> *Our God is in heaven; he does whatever pleases him. (Ps. 115:3)*

> *Who has measured the waters in the hollow of his hand, or with the breadth of his hand marked off the heavens? Who has held the dust*

of the earth in a basket, or weighed the mountains on the scales and the hills in a balance? (Is. 40:12)

He determines the number of the stars and calls them each by name. Great is our Lord and mighty in power; his understanding has no limit. (Ps. 147:4-5)

Therefore God exalted him to the highest place and gave him the name that is above every name, that at the name of Jesus every knee should bow, in heaven and on earth and under the earth, and every tongue confess that Jesus Christ is Lord, to the glory of God the Father. (Phil. 2:9-11)

He is the image of the invisible God, the firstborn over all creation. For by him all things were created: things in heaven and on earth, visible and invisible, whether thrones or powers or rulers or authorities; all things were created by him and for him. He is before all things, and in him all things hold together. (Col. 1:15-17)

As troublesome as Satan is, he is not a problem to God. As a mere created being, his power cannot even be compared to God's. When Satan rose up in pride, he was instantly cast out of heaven (Luke 10:18).

The great battles that take place are not because God is fighting to gain victory, but because God has ordained that victories are won through the prayers and perseverance of His people as they grow in Him (Eph. 3:10). As Christians, we represent the kingdom of the Almighty God and are commanded and commissioned to confront the powers of darkness in the name of Jesus without fear.

STUDY QUESTIONS

1. Why is the greatness of God the necessary context for a study on Satan, fallen angels and demons?
2. Suggest some reasons why God, who reigns supreme, would allow evil to continue.

The Origin and Nature of Satan

Isaiah 14 and Ezekiel 28 contain very significant prophecies, each of which can be understood on three levels:

- The prophets pronounce judgment against two temporal rulers: the king of Babylon in Isaiah 14, and the king of the wealthy seaport city of Tyre in Ezekiel 28.
- These temporal rulers also prophetically foreshadow the antichrist of the Last Days. He too will be the enemy of God's people, and will be destroyed by God.
- In this context, the prophecies also address Satan himself – the spirit behind both the temporal rulers and the Antichrist.

Thus, these prophecies go beyond their human subjects and actually describe the origin, original position, sin and fall of Satan.

> *How you are fallen from heaven, O Lucifer, son of the morning! How you are cut down to the ground, You who weakened the nations! For you have said in your heart: "I will ascend into heaven, I will exalt my throne above the stars of God; I will also sit on the mount of the congregation On the farthest sides of the north; I will ascend above the heights of the clouds, I will be like the Most High." Yet you shall be brought down to Sheol, To the lowest depths of the Pit. (Is. 14:12-15, NKJV)*

Son of man, take up a lamentation for the king of Tyre, and say to him, "Thus says the Lord GOD: 'You were the seal of perfection, Full of wisdom and perfect in beauty. You were in Eden, the garden of God; Every precious stone was your covering: The sardius, topaz, and diamond, Beryl, onyx, and jasper, Sapphire, turquoise, and emerald with gold. The workmanship of your timbrels and pipes Was prepared for you on the day you were created. You were the anointed cherub who covers; I established you; You were on the holy mountain of God; You walked back and forth in the midst of fiery stones. You were perfect in your ways from the day you were created, Till iniquity was found in you. By the abundance of your trading You became filled with violence within, And you sinned; Therefore I cast you as a profane thing Out of the mountain of God; And I destroyed you, O covering cherub, From the midst of the fiery stones. Your heart was lifted up because of your beauty; You corrupted your wisdom for the sake of your splendor; I cast you to the ground, I laid you before kings, That they might gaze at you.'" (Ezek. 28:12-17, NKJV)

From these and other passages, the following can be learned about the origin and history of Satan.

1. Satan was created.

> *...The workmanship of your timbrels and pipes Was prepared for you on the day you were created.* (Ezek. 28:13, NKJV)

God created all spiritual beings that exist. These include angels, cherubim, seraphim, Satan, and his entire host. Only God is eternal. God *is* Spirit, while Satan is *a* spirit. In stark contrast to God, Satan has all the finiteness of a created being.

- God is infinite. Satan is finite.
- God is omnipresent. Satan is limited to one place at a time (although he can move quickly from place to place, and he does have many demons working with him).

- God is omnipotent. Satan's power, though great in comparison to human ability, is limited.
- God is omniscient. Satan's knowledge is limited.

The Eastern philosophy of good and evil as eternally equal, but opposite, forces is completely at odds with the truth presented in Scripture.

2. **Satan was created good.**

   You were perfect in your ways from the day you were created, Till iniquity was found in you. (Ezek. 28:15, NKJV)

   He was created perfect. His original name Lucifer means "Light-bearer." Everything that God originally created was good (Gen. 1:31); it was not possible for God to create anything that was not good!

   How could a perfect being existing in the indescribable glory of the presence of Almighty God possibly sin? Somehow the capacity to obey and worship God from the heart makes obedience and worship a choice. Satan at some point chose sin.

3. **Satan was likely the highest created being. He was very powerful, very wise, and very beautiful.**

   …You were the seal of perfection, Full of wisdom and perfect in beauty. (Ezek. 28:12, NKJV)

   He was "the anointed cherub who covers" (Ezek. 28:14). The position of the cherubim above the ark of the covenant in the tabernacle of Moses, a shadow of the reality in heaven, suggests that these beings are the very closest to the manifest presence of God. Perhaps the replacement of the one cherub who fell, with two cherubim who constantly saw one another (Ex. 25:18-20), was meant to remove the possibility of uniqueness becoming a source of pride again. It also established accountability between them.

4. **Satan was very musical.**

   > ...*The workmanship of your timbrels and pipes Was prepared for you on the day you were created. (Ezek. 28:13)*

   Music has great spiritual power for good or evil. Anointed music draws us into worship and the presence of God. Satan still uses music, but now he uses it for the purpose of drawing hearts away from God and to worship himself.

5. **Satan's heart was lifted up in pride (1 Tim. 3:6). He responded to the gifts God had given him with five rebellious "I wills".**

   > *For you have said in your heart: "I will ascend into heaven, I will exalt my throne above the stars of God; I will also sit on the mount of the congregation On the farthest sides of the north; I will ascend above the heights of the clouds, I will be like the Most High." (Is. 14:13-14, NKJV)*

   Thus, self-will, rebellion, pride, and independence are at the very heart of all sin. Godliness is the exact opposite of all these and involves love for God (John 14:21), the full turning of the heart's attention toward Him (cf. John 1:1) and entire dependence on Him (cf. John 5:19).

6. **Satan not only wanted God's authority, but he also wanted worship. He wanted to be like the Most High. Today he receives worship indirectly at the hands of those who are in any form of idolatry, which includes covetousness and greed (Col. 3:5). We all worship either God or Satan. There is no middle ground for those who just want to live for themselves. This has been the great choice of the ages: who will man worship? God or Satan?**

   In the Last Days, Satan through deception will briefly gain his long-coveted worldwide worship:

> *All inhabitants of the earth will worship the beast – all whose names have not been written in the book of life belonging to the Lamb that was slain from the creation of the world. (Rev. 13:8)*

7. God cast him down. His expulsion from the garden of God was immediate. Jesus said, "I saw Satan fall like lightning from heaven" (Luke 10:18).

> *…And you sinned; Therefore I cast you as a profane thing Out of the mountain of God; And I destroyed you, O covering cherub, From the midst of the fiery stones. (Ezek. 28:16)*

His original name, Lucifer, meant "shining one" or "light-bearer." He then became known as Satan (lit. adversary), or "the devil."

SATAN'S MANY NAMES

Satan's nature and work are revealed in the various names that are used throughout Scripture to describe him. Some of his names are:

- Satan = adversary; one who is hostile, in opposition, against. In Hebrew, "satan" is the simple word for adversary (e.g., Num. 22:22; 1 Sam. 29:4; 1 Kings 11:25), but it came to be the particular name of the devil (e.g., 1 Chron. 21:1; Job 1:6; Zech. 3:1).
- Devil = false accuser, slanderer (Matt. 4:1).
- Serpent: describes his deceptive nature (Rev. 20:2). Images of a powerful serpent are found in the culture of the Australian aborigines.
- Dragon: powerful and evil (Rev. 12:9). Dragons are common in China as symbols of "good luck"!
- Abaddon or Apollyon = Destroyer (Rev. 9:11).
- Belial = perverse, worthless (1 Sam. 2:12 KJV).
- Beelzebub = lord of the flies (Matt. 12:24).
- Appears as an "angel of light": highlights his religious deception (2 Cor. 11:14).

- Enemy or adversary (1 Pet. 5:8).
- Oppressor (Acts 10:38).
- Accuser of the brethren (Job 1:9-11; Rev. 12:10).
- Murderer (John 8:44).
- Liar and the father of lies (John 8:44).
- Deceiver (2 John 7).
- Tempter (Matt. 4:3).

THE PRESENT POSITION OF SATAN

The Scriptures describe Satan as the "god" of this age and the "prince" of this world.

> *The god of this age has blinded the minds of unbelievers, so that they cannot see the light of the gospel of the glory of Christ, who is the image of God. (2 Cor. 4:4)*
>
> *I will not speak with you much longer, for the prince of this world is coming. He has no hold on me, (John 14:30)*
>
> *Again, the devil took him to a very high mountain and showed him all the kingdoms of the world and their splendor. "All this I will give you," he said, "if you will bow down and worship me." (Matt. 4:8-9)*

As at his fall from heaven, Satan's consuming desire is to be worshiped in the place of God. As ruler of this world, Satan seeks to blind men and women to the truth of the Gospel of Jesus Christ, and to usurp the worship that belongs to God alone. His goal is to prevent or destroy true worship and true worshipers (2 Cor. 11:3). Consequently, he will focus his hostility on believers who are actively spreading the Word of God.

Satan does not possess independent authority, but he has exercised special influence and activities here on earth since the time of Adam's fall. Throughout the centuries, he has been allowed to harass and oppress the inhabitants of the earth. When God is finished with him, He will dispose of him (Rev. 20:1-3, 7-10).

God is the ultimate God and Ruler over all and Satan can only go as far as He allows. God Almighty has the final say in human affairs. This is clearly seen in the account of Job. Satan was required to obtain permission from God before carrying out the destruction of Job's family, property and health (Job 1:12; 2:6). Satan's activity was limited by God, and was ultimately used to bring promotion and blessing to Job and glory to God. Our spiritual battles produce the same results as we endure by faith.

> *Consider it pure joy, my brothers, whenever you face trials of many kinds, because you know that the testing of your faith develops perseverance. Perseverance must finish its work so that you may be mature and complete, not lacking anything. (James 1:2-4)*

From his side, Satan is doing what he wants to do, but in reality, he is fulfilling the purpose of God!

This principle is restated in 1 Corinthians 10:13.

> *No temptation has seized you except what is common to man. And God is faithful; he will not let you be tempted beyond what you can bear. But when you are tempted, he will also provide a way out so that you can stand up under it.*

If Satan were autonomous, we would have reason to be afraid of him. However, God is always in complete control of all Satan's activities, fulfilling His own purposes. Since we know that God is sovereign over all, we can have strong confidence in all the circumstances of life, however difficult they may become.

THE DWELLING PLACE OF SATAN

The Scriptures describe three realms called "heavens":

1. **The first heaven. This is the physical atmosphere.**

    And God called the firmament Heaven… (Gen. 1:8, NKJV)

2. **The second heaven. The spiritual realm known as the second heaven is the present abiding place of Satan and the fallen angels.**

    For our struggle is not against flesh and blood, but against the rulers, against the authorities, against the powers of this dark world and against the spiritual forces of evil in the heavenly realms. (Eph. 6:12)

    This realm does not belong to Satan, but his influence is acknowledged in Scripture in his title of "the ruler of the kingdom of the air" (Eph. 2:2).

3. **The third heaven. This is the realm of God's glorious manifest presence.**

    I know a man in Christ who fourteen years ago was caught up to the third heaven. Whether it was in the body or out of the body I do not know – God knows. And I know that this man – whether in the body or apart from the body I do not know, but God knows – was caught up to paradise. He heard inexpressible things, things that man is not permitted to tell. (2 Cor. 12:2-4; cf. Luke 23:43)

    Satan has limited access to the throne of God when God permits:

    One day the angels came to present themselves before the LORD, and Satan also came with them. (Job 1:6; cf. 2:1; 1 Kings 22:19-22; Zech. 3:1)

The present abiding place of Satan is not hell:

> *Be self-controlled and alert. Your enemy the devil prowls around like a roaring lion looking for someone to devour. (1 Pet. 5:8)*

The devil may have access to hell as God allows. Nevertheless, hell will certainly never be his kingdom. Hell is the place God has prepared for sinful men (Is. 30:33). Satan will never be the "lord over hell"; he himself will suffer for eternity in hell under God's judgment.

> *Then he will say to those on his left, "Depart from me, you who are cursed, into the eternal fire prepared for the devil and his angels." (Matt. 25:41)*

SATAN'S ARMY

Satan was not alone in his rebellion against God. Many types of spiritual beings joined him and now share in his sentence of impending doom.

> *Then another sign appeared in heaven: an enormous red dragon with seven heads and ten horns and seven crowns on his heads. His tail swept a third of the stars out of the sky and flung them to the earth… (Rev. 12:3-4)*

This suggests that one third of the angelic beings defected to Satan and were cast out with him. If this is correct, not only is God infinitely more powerful than Satan, but there are also twice as many angels in God's army than Satan's! Furthermore, not all of Satan's followers at this time are free to work their evil.

Some are already in a place of confinement awaiting final judgment:

> *And the angels who did not keep their positions of authority but abandoned their own home – these he has kept in darkness, bound with everlasting chains for judgment on the great Day. (Jude 6)*

Others are bound until the time appointed for their release as a part of God's plan:

> *[The voice] said to the sixth angel who had the trumpet, "Release the four angels who are bound at the great river Euphrates." And the four angels who had been kept ready for this very hour and day and month and year were released to kill a third of mankind. (Rev. 9:14-15)*

Many others are active at present under Satan's rule. These beings, ranging from fallen angels to the lower order of evil spirits known as demons, all possess the same evil nature as their leader.

The wicked beings of Satan's kingdom exercise varying degrees of authority.

> *For our struggle is not against flesh and blood, but against the rulers, against the authorities, against the powers of this dark world and against the spiritual forces of evil in the heavenly realms. (Eph. 6:12)*

Paul did not write this verse as an exhaustive list to categorize all wicked spirits and define a precise theology concerning them. Rather, this is a general revelation of the diversity, organization, and hierarchy or rank of fallen spirit beings with whom we wrestle in our lives and ministries.

The concept of degrees of authority is also affirmed in the Book of Daniel:

> *...the prince of the Persian kingdom resisted me twenty-one days...(Dan. 10:13)*

SATAN'S TACTICS

It is a mistake to attribute unlimited power to Satan. Most of his destructive plans never come to pass (Ps. 21:11). In fact, power belongs to God (Ps. 62:11, NKJV), not Satan, and whatever he is able to do, he does because it is allowed for a purpose.

Man is created in the image of God (1 Cor. 11:7; Jam. 3:9), and though marred by sin, there is still a limited potential for some good. The image of God within is why people appreciate beauty, honor sacrifice, give to the needs of others, etc. On the other hand, the hearts of sinful humanity are darkened by sin, blind to truth, easily deceived, and committed to self-advancement. Satan has a fertile field for opposing God. Thus, mankind becomes the battleground. God is the Redeemer, calling out through His messengers for man to turn and live. Satan uses his evil tactics to enslave individuals and nations to their own lusts, bringing people and nations into alignment with him and keeping them in a state of broken fellowship with God, who alone saves.

Satan and his demonic forces have an arsenal of weapons of deception through which they seek to harm people. Even a believer can fall to these tactics if he is not clothed in the full armor of God and walking in truth. These tactics often prey upon the weakness of the flesh, pride, or other aspects of fallen nature or unsubmitted carnality. Much can be written about each tactic, but for our purposes, we will only introduce several of the most common and destructive.

Lies and Deceit. Jesus identified Satan as the father of lies (John 8:44). His first victory over mankind was through deceit.

> …The woman said, "The serpent deceived me, and I ate." (Gen. 3:13)

Satan didn't have the power to destroy Adam and Eve or to force them to disobey God, so he used deception, casting doubt on God's love and promising grand advancement and fulfillment. Through his trickery,

Satan lured the first couple into a disobedient act that broke their fellowship with God and brought them under His judgment.

When Satan uses this same tactic today, only after the damage is done is the lie exposed, but by then the heart is hardened and shamed and may drive the victim of the lie further from God.

A lie can be a powerful weapon, and, not surprisingly, the biggest lies of the enemy are set against the truth of God's Word. For the unbeliever, this may be offering a substitute for God, an idol that promises salvation and blessing but delivers either nothing or minimal blessing at a huge cost.

It is important for the believer to examine himself in the light of the Word of God to identify any lies that he is inadvertently holding on to. We must sever any agreement with the lies of the enemy regardless of how dear they may seem to us if we want to walk in the freedom Jesus died to give us.

Accusation, Shame and Condemnation. These related tactics are directed toward believers to turn their focus from redemption in Jesus' blood to their own sad condition apart from God's grace.

> *Then I heard a loud voice in heaven say, "Now have come the salvation and the power and the kingdom of our God, and the authority of his Christ. For the accuser of our brothers, who accuses them before our God day and night, has been hurled down." (Rev. 12:10)*

Zechariah chapter three opens with a vision of Joshua the high priest standing before the Angel of the Lord clothed in filthy garments, with Satan at his right hand opposing him. The Lord as Redeemer stands up for Joshua and rebukes Satan.

> *The angel said to those who were standing before him, "Take off his filthy clothes." Then he said to Joshua, "See, I have taken away your sin, and I will put rich garments on you." (Zech. 3:4)*

This is the glorious experience of believers, but sadly, many continue in shame even in the face of God's promise,

> *Therefore, there is now no condemnation for those who are in Christ Jesus, (Rom. 8:1)*

The strategy of shame and accusation is best applied to those who have a sensitive heart and truly want to be clean before God. As with other demonic tactics, shame is defeated by the truth of God's Word. Often, the help of a stronger brother or sister is needed for continuous encouragement to stand on the truth and reject feelings of worthlessness.

Temptation. Satan and his demon helpers are students of the human heart. They watch for weaknesses, and both legitimate and illegitimate desires. When the time is right, the enemy presents his case with such persuasion that our natural mind is very likely to give full agreement. Through temptation, Satan attempts to draw our focus away from God's glory and onto our own gain. The biblical account, as well as history and our own experience provide endless examples of Satan's success with temptation.

In the Gospel accounts of Jesus' temptation we see the strategy for breaking the power of temptation: "It is written…" (Matt. 4:4) Jesus gave us the example to battle the temptations (as well as lies and other strategies of the enemy) with the truth of the Word of God. In our own strength, wisdom, and desire to do right, we are no match for the cunning of Satan. We must apply ourselves to the Word of God, through which our minds and hearts are renewed as we actively believe and obey Him.

Intimidation and Fear. Satan rules through fear. Fear is a paralyzing emotional state that prevents rational thought. As mentioned earlier, Satan is not all-powerful and does not have the authorization to do all that he wants. But that doesn't stop him from making terrifying threats. Many false religions hold their people in obedience through fear.

The antidote to fear is trust in God and abandonment to Him. The believer has a hope in God through Jesus Christ that takes away even the fear of death, since death is not the final experience of the Christian. Jesus broke the enemy's power of death through His death and resurrection.

> *Since the children have flesh and blood, he too shared in their humanity so that by his death he might destroy him who holds the power of death – that is, the devil – and free those who all their lives were held in slavery by their fear of death. (Heb. 2:14-15)*

Curses. In counterfeiting the power of God's Word, the enemy uses empowered words through obedient human vessels to work damage and destruction. These vessels are not average sin-bound people, but those who have purposefully yielded themselves to Satan.

Usually they are directly involved in some Satanic or witchcraft community. Because of their close association with Satan, their words can carry spiritual power for evil.

Barak, the Moabite leader at the time of the Exodus, sought to use the power of cursing to prevent the people of Israel from conquering his land (Num. 22 – 24). This may have been a winning strategy, but God intervened and caused the words that Balaam uttered to be words of prophetic blessing instead of cursing.

> *However, the Lord your God would not listen to Balaam but turned the curse into a blessing for you, because the Lord your God loves you. (Deut. 23:5)*

> *Like a fluttering sparrow or a darting swallow, an undeserved curse does not come to rest. (Prov. 26:2)*

The curses of God that are pronounced upon the rebellious should be of much greater concern than the curses of a servant of Satan!

The above tactics are very effective on unbelievers. Sadly, they are often effective on believers as well. Satan uses these tactics to cause people (both unbelievers and believers, if they can be persuaded) to give place to him. From there, he has access to their lives. The unbeliever, throughout his lifetime, will doubtless open many doors to the devil, but the believer who knows God does not have to open doors. The enemy has no power over the one who abides in Christ and is clothed in the full armor of God.

> *We know that anyone born of God does not continue to sin; the one who was born of God keeps him safe, and the evil one cannot harm him. (1 John 5:18)*

SATAN'S DEFEAT AT THE CROSS

Jesus never had to defeat Satan for His own benefit. He always had complete authority and power over him. The victory of the cross was for us. Jesus defeated Satan on our behalf when He shed His blood to pay the penalty for our sin. Since the penalty for sin has been paid, Satan no longer has power over us.

Jesus did not defeat Satan in a battle. There was no dramatic "war in hell" as some Bible teachers describe. Jesus' death on the cross defeated Satan by providing an acceptable sacrifice which satisfied God's wrath against sin.

> *And I will put enmity Between you and the woman, And between your seed and her Seed; He shall bruise your head, And you shall bruise His heel. (Gen. 3:15, NKJV)*

In Genesis 3:15, the Gospel is preached for the first time. God revealed that there would arise a Man (the Seed of the woman) who would destroy the works of the devil, but in doing so He would have to die. In this verse God predicted and pledged, immediately after the Fall and for the first time in the Bible, that man would be reconciled to Himself; but in the course of His effecting that reconciliation, the heel of the woman's Seed would be "bruised." This is a clear prophetic reference to the death of Jesus on the cross.

> *Since the children have flesh and blood, he too shared in their humanity so that by his death he might destroy him who holds the power of death – that is, the devil – and free those who all their lives were held in slavery by their fear of death. (Heb. 2:14-15)*

Hebrews 2:14-15 teaches that it was through the death of Jesus' body, not through a battle, that the devil's "head" was "bruised." The Greek word translated "destroy" in this passage means "to reduce to inactivity" or "to bring to nought." This means that through the death of Jesus on the cross, the devil has been rendered powerless with respect to the redeemed. Notice also that the Greek text in this passage says that Satan "has"[1] the power of death. Some have taught that Satan "had" the power of death until Jesus beat him up in the pit of hell and took the power of death away from him. However, Paul says that Satan still "has" the power of death. God is still using the devil to reveal the hearts of men, to execute His righteous judgments against the sin of man, and also to mature His own saints. As we have seen, God uses the destructive nature of Satan to accomplish His own purposes.

> *… (God) graciously forgave us all our shortcomings, canceled the note that stood against us, with its requirements, and has put it out of our way by nailing it to the cross. He thus stripped the principalities and dominions of power and made a public display of them, triumphing over them by the cross. (Col. 2:13-15, Williams New Testament)*

Paul says, in Colossians 2:13-15, that it was at the cross – where Jesus shed His blood and died – that the demonic principalities and powers were stripped of their authority. Jesus did not redeem us from Satan's power through a battle in hell; He redeemed us by dying on the cross.

---

[1] The word used here is the present participle of the verb *echo:* "to have or to hold."

> "Now is the time for judgment on this world; now the prince of this world will be driven out. But I, when I am lifted up from the earth, will draw all men to myself." He said this to show the kind of death he was going to die. (John 12:31-33)

In John 12:31-33, Jesus taught that it was when He died on the cross that the prince or ruler of this world was "driven out." Satan was defeated at the cross by the shed blood of Jesus.

> They overcame him [Satan] by the blood of the Lamb... (Rev. 12:11)

Since the penalty for sin has been paid, Satan no longer has power over the believer. His authority has been annulled (Heb. 2:14-15).

SATAN'S END

Satan may appear powerful at present, but his downfall is certain. At the time appointed by the Father, Satan and his followers will be dealt with decisively in the justice of God. No plan of redemption or reconciliation exists for these evil spiritual beings. Satan and his entire host, including all the demon spirits, along with unredeemed humanity, will spend eternity in the Lake of Fire.

> "What do you want with us, Son of God?" they shouted. "Have you come here to torture us before the appointed time?" (Matt. 8:29)

> And the devil, who deceived them, was thrown into the lake of burning sulfur, where the beast and the false prophet had been thrown. They will be tormented day and night for ever and ever. (Rev. 20:10)

STUDY QUESTIONS

1. Name three contrasts between God and Satan.
2. What are some of Satan's goals?
3. How do people relate to Satan's goal?
4. Name two of Satan's most successful tactics.

The Origin and Nature of Demons

Demons are the lowest in the order of spiritual wickedness among the evil spirits, both in rank and location. Like their leader, they are fully evil and desire to express their corrupt nature through human hosts. These are the ones Satan directly uses to oppress individual lives and families and bring them into various kinds of bondages – spirit, soul, mind and body. Their purpose is summarized by Jesus:

> *The thief comes only to steal and kill and destroy… (John 10:10)*

THE ORIGIN OF DEMONS

The Bible is silent regarding the origin of demons (its main subject is God and His dealings with men), but several theories offer explanations:

- Demons are the disembodied spirits of a pre-Adamic race that existed before the creation of Genesis 1:3. This view is part of the abstruse "gap theory" which was popular some years ago but happily has fallen from favor. According to this theory, there was a "gap" between verses 1 and 2 of Genesis 1, during which time God created and then destroyed a "pre-Adamic race." This is speculation that is nowhere taught in the Scriptures.

- Demons are the result of the union between fallen angels and mortal women mentioned in the sixth chapter of Genesis.
- Demons are angelic creatures who fell with Satan. This is the simplest and most logical view, and has no real theological problems.

DEMONS HAVE PERSONALITY

The Scriptures describe demons as intelligent and personal spirit beings. They are not ancient superstitions or mere psychological conditions that affect people's lives. Neither are they mere "spiritual robots." They are beings with individual personalities, just as the holy angels are. They display various characteristics of personality such as self-awareness, will, knowledge, emotion and speech.

- Self-awareness:

    He shouted at the top of his voice, "What do you want with me, Jesus, Son of the Most High God? Swear to God that you won't torture me!" For Jesus had said to him, "Come out of this man, you evil spirit!" Then Jesus asked him, "What is your name?" "My name is Legion," he replied, "for we are many." (Mark 5:7-9)

    The spirit knew who it was. Every demon knows who it is and what its function is.

    Finally, a spirit came forward, stood before the LORD and said, "I will entice him." "By what means?" the LORD asked. "I will go out and be a lying spirit in the mouths of all his prophets," he said... (1 Kings 22:21-22)

- Will:

    When an evil spirit comes out of a man, it goes through arid places seeking rest and does not find it. Then it says, "I will return to the house I left." When it arrives, it finds the house unoccupied, swept clean and put in order. Then it goes and takes with it seven other spirits more wicked than itself, and they go in and live there. And the final condition of that man is worse than the first... (Matt. 12:43-45)

During the ministry of deliverance it is not uncommon for a demon to declare, "I will not come out. This is my house. I've been here for many years, and I'm not leaving!" Of course, he must leave, but his protest is an expression of will.

- Knowledge:

    Now there was a man in their synagogue with an unclean spirit. And he cried out, saying, "Let us alone! What have we to do with You, Jesus of Nazareth? Did You come to destroy us? I know who You are; the Holy One of God!" (Mark 1:23-24, NKJV)

    Here the demon knew Jesus and reacted defensively.

    ...the evil spirit answered them, "Jesus I know, and I know about Paul, but who are you?" (Acts 19:15)

    Not only do these evil spirits know about Jesus and the apostles, but they know about you. There have been cases when someone was trying to cast a demon out of another person and the demon spoke and revealed some of his sins! Of course, that undermined his authority a little! As the sons of Sceva also proved (Acts 19:13-16), it is not sufficient to merely repeat the right formula for deliverance. You must possess genuine authority in the spiritual realm.

- Emotion:

    As evil beings, they display only negative or destructive emotions. The demonic realm is completely devoid of love.

> *You believe that there is one God. Good! Even the demons believe that – and shudder. (Jam. 2:19)*

Demons can display fear. They can also become violent (cf. Acts 19:16). There have been times when demons have tried to physically attack those casting them out, attempting to strangle them or pick their eyes out. On other occasions, the demons have cried, "I'm going to kill you" to the one ministering deliverance. Of course, if the demon were able to kill the person, it would have done so a long time ago!

- Expression:

> *Whenever the evil spirits saw him, they fell down before him and cried out, "You are the Son of God." (Mark 3:11)*

In this passage, the demon expressed itself through speech and prostration. Demons can be very expressive, especially in the presence of the anointing of the Holy Spirit. Many times when the Holy Spirit is moving powerfully in a meeting, demons are stirred up as well, and influence people to do strange things that distract people from God's purposes of repentance and faith. It is important for believers to remember that a spiritual influence is not necessarily the Holy Spirit. If it's weird, out of control and draws attention to the person, it's probably not of God. We must remember that "the spirits of prophets are subject to the control of prophets" (1 Cor. 14:32).

THE PRESENT LOCATION OF DEMONS

Demons are distinct from fallen angels who abide in the second heaven. Demons look upon people's lives as their homes.

> *When an evil spirit comes out of a man, it goes through arid places seeking rest and does not find it. Then it says, "I will return to the*

house I left." When it arrives, it finds the house unoccupied, swept clean and put in order. (Matt. 12:43-44)

Demons dwell in our terrestrial realm seeking out living beings, people in particular (but sometimes animals or objects), through which to express themselves. They can afflict physically, emotionally, mentally and spiritually.

Moreover, demons can become so intertwined in the personality of an individual, that the person doesn't know the difference between their own thoughts and thought processes and those of the demon. If left undisturbed, demon oppression will pass from generation to generation in a family line.

THE FORM OF DEMONS

Demons are spirits and normally cannot be seen with natural eyes. Occasionally, however, some people will see demons. Their appearance differs according to their rank.

Higher-level fallen angels can appear in human form. One man saw a high-ranking demon that appeared in the form of a well-dressed, middle-aged man. Another woman saw a human figure with eyes of fire.

In order to gain influence and deceive, evil spirits can appear in strikingly beautiful forms:

…Satan himself masquerades as an angel of light. (2 Cor. 11:14)

Farther down the scale, evil spirits can be of mixed forms, for example half human and half animal. Many mythical figures such as mermaids (half woman, half fish), satyrs (half man, half goat), and centaurs (half man, half horse) are actually representations of demons. The lowest demons have animal forms and forms that would be unrecognizable to us.

> *I have given you authority to trample on snakes and scorpions and to overcome all the power of the enemy; nothing will harm you. (Luke 10:19)*
>
> *Then I saw three evil spirits that looked like frogs; they came out of the mouth of the dragon, out of the mouth of the beast and out of the mouth of the false prophet. (Rev. 16:13)*

Those with the gift of discerning of spirits have seen evil spirits as snakes, frogs, monkeys and spiders, as well as other strange and hideous forms. Many temples of false religions around the world are adorned with grotesque images – statues and symbolic objects – that represent the demons that are worshiped there. Sadly, children are often targeted for exposure to the likeness of demons in the form of characters in fairy tales, toys, and children's films.

DEMONS AND SPIRITUAL AUTHORITY

As we have seen in Ephesians 6:12, Satan has a highly organized kingdom of fallen spirit beings. They have different functions and exercise varying degrees of authority and power.

The ministry of deliverance specifically involves deliverance from the activity and influence of demon spirits. Demons are a low level of spirit being in Satan's kingdom. Their role is to oppress people and bring them into various kinds of bondages – spirit, soul, mind, and body. Once established in a human, demons are extremely reluctant to leave and must be evicted by force: "…if I drive out demons by the Spirit of God…" (Matt. 12:28).

In Christ, we have positional superiority of authority over all the ranks of Satan's kingdom (Eph. 1:20-21, 2:5-6). This means we need not fear principalities and powers as we carry out the work of the Kingdom of God anywhere on earth, but it does not mean we can decide to tear down territorial principalities whenever we think they are in our way (as one Chinese leader asked, "Where would they go if you did pull them down?"). We are not specifically authorized to deal with the higher ranks of evil spirits.

A child in a family is an heir and partaker of all the blessings and resources of his family. Although – theoretically and positionally – he is the heir of all his father owns, that does not mean he can go and buy a new car with his parent's credit card! He is not authorized to do that. He is, however, authorized to keep his room clean, and he should need no further instruction or authorization to do that.

Revelation 20:1-3 predicts the time when an angel from God will come down from heaven, bind Satan with a great chain and cast him into the bottomless pit for 1000 years. Why does the angel not do this before this time? Although this holy angel is obviously capable of binding Satan now, God has not yet authorized him to do so. Having positional authority is one thing; being authorized by God to use it is another.

Similarly, there is neither command nor precedent in Scripture for casting out evil principalities from heavenly regions or from over cities.

Paul's statement in Ephesians 6:12 that we "struggle… against the rulers, against the authorities, against the powers of this dark world and against the spiritual forces of evil in the heavenly realms" is not a commandment to hold prayer meetings to cast principalities out of heaven, but it is a recognition of the fact that as we serve God and do the work of the ministry we are engaging in a spiritual warfare with unseen foes. Significantly, the several specific mentions of prayer in Ephesians 6:18-20 all involve the work of the Gospel; there is no mention of tearing down territorial principalities or even directly addressing them. If Paul had wanted us to do that, this would have been the perfect place for him to say so.

Consider the context of the revelation of the demonic "prince of Persia" in Daniel 10. Daniel was not praying to pull it down. He was praying for his people and for the revelation of God's will. But as he did the work of his ministry, in the spiritual realm a great battle took place. Daniel did not personally take part in this battle by directly praying against the prince of Persia – the battle was fought in response to his prayer for his people.

In the same way, our battle against principalities and powers in the heavenly realms is not accomplished by calling prayer meetings to tear those spirits down, but we engage in this battle as we preach the Gospel, plant churches, pray for God's will to be accomplished and otherwise do the work of the ministry.

Moreover, there is no scriptural evidence that Jesus Himself ever directly or intentionally confronted territorial principalities and powers. Quite the opposite is true. When Jesus cast the powerful evil spirits out of the Gadarene demoniac in Mark 5, the spirits specifically asked not to be sent out of the territory:

> *And he begged Jesus again and again not to send them out of the area. (Mark 5:10)*

Amazingly, Jesus conceded and did not send them out of the territory but allowed them to enter the herd of pigs (Mark 5:13). Thus, Jesus did not contravene the territorial nature of the evil spirits' assignments. The Father had not instructed Him to do that (John 5:19). If Jesus did not "pick fights" with territorial spirits without the Father's specific command, how much less should we?

A more profitable way to pray is with "replacement prayers." For example, instead of casting down principalities of pride, we can ask God to replace the pride in our city with humility. Instead of coming against the principalities of pornography, we can ask God to pour out His Holy Spirit upon a region, bringing repentance and holiness.

Although believers are not given free reign to come against evil principalities and powers, we are commanded and given authority by Jesus to cast out demon spirits from individuals, and we need no additional instructions from God to do this.

> *He called his twelve disciples to him and gave them authority to drive out evil spirits and to heal every disease and sickness. (Matt. 10:1)*
>
> *Heal the sick, raise the dead, cleanse those who have leprosy, drive out demons. Freely you have received, freely give. (Matt. 10:8)*
>
> *And these signs will accompany those who believe: In my name they will drive out demons... (Mark 16:17)*

There are examples in the gospels and the Book of Acts of believers carrying out this command:

> *The seventy-two returned with joy and said, "Lord, even the demons submit to us in your name." (Luke 10:17)*
>
> *When the crowds heard Philip and saw the miraculous signs he did, they all paid close attention to what he said. With shrieks, evil spirits came out of many, and many paralytics and cripples were healed. (Acts 8:6-7)*
>
> *...Finally Paul became so troubled that he turned around and said to the spirit, "In the name of Jesus Christ I command you to come out of her!" At that moment the spirit left her. (Acts 16:18)*

Jesus gave us authority to cast out demons. That is what we should do – and we need no additional authorization regarding it – but we should leave the principalities and powers to God.

Furthermore, it is neither necessary nor advisable to be specific as to directing where expelled demons are to go. There is no example or command in Scripture to "put them in boxes" or send them to hell, or anywhere else. Jesus said they will go to the dry places, but He didn't tell us to command them to go there. The only additional directive Jesus ever made was that a demon not return:

"You deaf and mute spirit," he said, *"I command you, come out of him and never enter him again." (Mark 9:25)*

NAMES OF DEMONS

The specific destructive function of an individual demon is revealed by its name. Names of demons mentioned in the Bible include:

- Evil spirit (Jud. 9:23; 1 Sam. 18:10; 19:9; Acts 19:12).
- Unclean spirit (Zech. 13:2; Matt. 10:1; Mark 9:25; Rev. 18:2).
- Deaf and dumb spirit (Mark 9:25).
- Spirit of infirmity (Luke 13:11).
- Lying spirit (1 Kings 22:22; 2 Chron. 18:21-22).
- A familiar spirit in a medium (Lev. 19:31, KJV; 20:6, KJV; 1 Chron. 10:13, KJV).
- Perverse spirit – a "spirit of dizziness" in NIV, causing distorted judgment (Is. 19:14, KJV).
- Spirit of divination (Acts 16:16).
- Spirit of harlotry (Hos. 5:4).
- Seducing spirits, also known as religious or deceiving spirits (1 Tim. 4:1).
- Spirit of fear (2 Tim. 1:7).

We should be wary of teachings that give explicit names for demons apart from any Scriptural basis. In the Bible, the demons named are called by the name of a particular problem or condition. They are not called "Bill," or "Fred." They are described or named according to their natures.

Knowing the name of a demon is helpful because it gives you focus in prayer. There are several ways to determine names:

- The person afflicted usually knows in what area of life he is bound.
- God may reveal the name through a word of knowledge.
- As you pray for a person's deliverance, ask questions such as:

"Is it out?"
"What do we need to address now?"
"What are you feeling now?"
The reply may give great insight in directing your commands.

- A demon may speak its name through a severely oppressed individual when asked.

    Then Jesus asked him, "What is your name?" "My name is Legion," he replied, "for we are many." (Mark 5:9)

Knowing the demon's name will help to give you focus in prayer, but you don't have to know its name. If a specific name is not known, cast the demon out anyway. A demon can be addressed in a generic fashion, such as "spirit causing this condition" or even as "Satan" whom it represents. The spirit knows you are speaking to it and it must respond to your authority in Christ, even if you do not address it by its exact name.

The Bible names many kinds of demons, and there are many more. Nevertheless, it is a mistake to attribute every unpleasant circumstance or condition to a demon. The works of the flesh listed in Galatians 5, as aberrant as they are, are not ascribed to demons.

Not every negative emotion or feeling one may have is caused by a demon. For example, you may feel grief at the loss of a relative, but that doesn't mean you have a spirit of grief. Grief is a normal human emotion. In contrast, an obsessive, tormenting grief that persists is demonic. Similarly, fear is a normal human mechanism that can motivate us to caution and self-preservation, but a driving tormenting fear is a spirit.

GROUPINGS OF DEMONS

Vast numbers of demons go about their task of oppressing and destroying lives. Revelation 5:11 describes the vast numbers of angels who are before God's throne:

> *Then I looked and heard the voice of many angels, numbering thousands upon thousands, and ten thousand times ten thousand. They encircled the throne and the living creatures and the elders.*

If one third of all spirit beings are fallen (Rev. 12:3-4), that means there are many demons!

"My name is Legion, for we are many," said the spokesman spirit in Mark 5:9. A legion was a military unit of the Roman army comprising three to six thousand men. Therefore, this one man had thousands of evil spirits in him! Jesus then cast them out and, with His permission, they entered into a herd of 2000 pigs and drove them over the cliff into the lake.

While most cases of oppression are not that severe, it is very common to have many spirits at work in an individual. Evil spirits increase the strength of their hold through greater numbers. The more demons of lust in a person, the greater the hold of lust on the person's life. Deliverance may take longer in areas of stronger bondage where multiple spirits are involved, simply because there are more to be cast out. Sometimes, a person may receive some genuine deliverance in one area of life, but then experience a reoccurrence of the same problems. This may simply mean that there are more of the same kind of demon to be cast out. So, don't be discouraged – cast them out!

Generally, multiple spirits oppressing an individual work together in groups, or families of spirits. For example, a person with a spirit of fear may have various kinds of spirits of fear, such as fear of man, fear of failure, fear of authority, etc. A spirit (or spirits) of fear may be accompanied by spirits of anxiety, inferiority, or other related conditions. A person with a spirit of rejection often has fear of rejection and anger as oppressing spirits. This deadly combination often opens doors to depression and suicide, as well.

When Jesus drove "seven demons" out of Mary Magdalene (Mark 16:9) it was probably seven families of spirits.

Because demons work in groups, it is best when dealing with them to speak in the singular, but think in the plural. In the gospels, a group of spirits can be referred to either as "a spirit" or "spirits". The interchange of singular and plural is seen in Mark 1:23-26 and Mark 5:2-13.

> *Just then a man in their synagogue who was possessed by an **evil spirit** cried out, "What do you want with **us**, Jesus of Nazareth? Have you come to destroy **us?** I know who you are – the Holy One of God!" "Be quiet!" said Jesus sternly. "Come out of him!" **The evil spirit** shook the man violently and came out of him with a shriek. (Mark 1:23-26)*

> *… a man with **an evil spirit**… He shouted at the top of his voice, "What do you want with **me**, Jesus, Son of the Most High God? Swear to God that you won't torture **me!**" For Jesus had said to **him**, "Come out of this man, you evil **spirit!**" Then Jesus asked **him**, "What is your name?" "**My** name is Legion," he replied, "for **we** are many." And **he** begged Jesus again and again not to send **them** out of the area. A large herd of pigs was feeding on the nearby hillside. The **demons** begged Jesus, "Send **us** among the pigs; allow **us** to go into them." He gave **them** permission, and the evil **spirits** came out and went into the pigs. (Mark 5:2-13)*

Often there is a spokesman spirit that exercises more power and control than other spirits and controls the activity of other spirits. This is referred to in the gospels as the "strongman." When this demon is exposed and cast out, remaining demons leave with less resistance.

> *But if I cast out demons by the Spirit of God, surely the kingdom of God has come upon you. Or how can one enter a strong man's house and plunder his goods, unless he first bind the strong man? (Matt. 12:28-29).*

THE DEFEAT AND FINAL DESTINY OF DEMONS

The demons, along with Satan himself, were defeated at the cross by the shed blood of Jesus. Their final destination is the eternal lake of fire with Satan and unredeemed humanity. Once there, demons will not be administering torment to unbelievers. Neither will they be enjoying some big "party" in hell, but all will be suffering indescribable agonies and torments forever for their sins.

> *"What do you want with us, Son of God?" they shouted. "Have you come here to torture us before the appointed time?" (Matt. 8:29)*

> *Then he will say to those on his left, "Depart from me, you who are cursed, into the eternal fire prepared for the devil and his angels." (Matt. 25:41)*

STUDY QUESTIONS

1. What do demons have in common?
2. What can be gained by learning the name of a demon?
3. How does casting a demon out of a person differ from dealing with principalities over cities and regions?
4. What is the difference between the works of the flesh and the work of a demon?

The Christian and Deliverance

There is considerable controversy in the church regarding whether or not a Christian can have a demon. The arguments typically advanced against the idea of a Christian having a demon are as follows:

1. **"The believer is inhabited by the Holy Spirit; therefore the demons cannot coexist in the same body or spirit."**

    The error of this is demonstrated simply by the observation that, in one sense, the whole universe is "filled" with the Holy Spirit (Jer. 23:24, Ps. 139:7-10), and yet that does not mean Satan cannot coexist in the universe. Spirits do not occupy space like material beings do. Spirits are not subject to the limitations of space, and more than one spirit being can inhabit the same physical location.

2. **"If Jesus is Lord of the believer's life, how could a demon be in the person?"**

    However, according to this same logic: if Jesus is Lord of the believer's life, how could the believer ever sin? The fact that a person is saved does not automatically relieve him of the responsibility to deliberately walk in the Spirit on the one hand (Gal. 5:16), and to resist the devil on the other (Jam. 4:7). Victory over sin in the believer's life is not automatic; neither is deliverance from the devil. Jesus purchased the believer with His own blood and made him a steward over his own life. The devil has no legal right to him, but it is up to the believer to defend his rights (1 John 5:18).

3. **"The struggle inside the believer in the New Testament is always revealed to be the struggle between the flesh and the Spirit, and not a struggle involving demons (Romans 6 and 7)."**

This argument ignores the fact that deliverance was an integral part of the preaching of the Gospel in the first century, and the New Testament church practiced deliverance when people got saved (Mark 16:15-17). Thus, in the epistles Paul emphasizes crucifying the flesh, presupposing that the believer has already been delivered from demonic oppression. But even with this emphasis, many passages give clear commands for the believer to continue to resist Satan (1 Pet. 5:8-9; Jam. 4:7).

4. **"The believer is delivered from the power of Satan and his demons (Colossians 1:12-13; Ephesians 2:1-3)."**

Certainly this is true legally, but it does not happen automatically in the believer's life. On this side of eternity, we must daily walk with the Lord Jesus in obedience and faith, and meet the conditions for the victorious life. It does not happen to us spontaneously. Just as a believer, whom Jesus Christ has delivered from sin (Rom. 6:18), can still be bound by sin in his life, so he can still be bound by a demon in his life. John Wimber (1987, p. 116) wrote, "Our situation with demons is analogous to our situation with the flesh and the world. We are forgiven and born again in Christ, but if we choose to believe the lies of the world and yield to our flesh, we will live in sin. Demonization works the same way: we have been delivered from the power of demons, yet we can still be affected by them."

THE SCRIPTURAL EVIDENCE

Believers cannot be possessed in the sense of "owned" by demons or "filled to capacity" with demons, but it is possible for a believer to be demonized. The Scriptures give a number of illustrations.

In the Old Testament, King Saul was a believer who had been anointed by the Holy Spirit and had even prophesied (1 Sam. 10:1, 9-13). But after Saul sinned, he was tormented by an evil spirit (1 Sam. 16:14). As a result of this oppression, and his own sin, Saul was given to fits of anger, murder and fear, and eventually fell prey to the sins of witchcraft and suicide, all of which may be characteristics of a demonized person.

There are many instances of believers being oppressed by demons in the New Testament. One of the most noteworthy is the account in Luke 13:10-16, of the woman Jesus delivered from "a spirit of infirmity." Jesus defended his actions by identifying the woman as a "daughter of Abraham" – that is, an heir to the promises, a believer at that time (cf. Luke 19:9; John 8:39; Gal. 3:7). His declaration, "Should not this woman, a daughter of Abraham, whom Satan has kept bound for eighteen long years, be set free…from what bound her?" (Luke 13:16) emphasizes the appropriateness of a believer living in freedom from bondage. Today, many Christians with physical infirmities receive healing when a demon is cast out.

Another notable illustration from Jesus' ministry is the account, in Mark 7:25-30, of the Syro-Phoenician woman who asked Jesus to give her oppressed daughter some "crumbs" from "the children's bread" of deliverance. If deliverance is the "bread" that belongs to the children of the covenant, then presumably they must need deliverance occasionally!

On several other occasions in the gospels, Jesus cast spirits out of believers. He "rebuked" the fever in Peter's mother-in-law, obviously addressing the spirit behind the sickness (Luke 4:38-39). Certainly this woman who served Jesus (Matt. 8:15) would have been a believer.

Furthermore, Jesus delivered a man in the synagogue from an unclean spirit in Mark 1:23-26. We have no reason to doubt that this man was a believer who had come to worship God there.

Presumably Judas was a believer at one time, and yet Satan himself "entered" him (Luke 22:3; cf. John 13:2).

Ananias and Sapphira were numbered among the believers mentioned in Acts 4:32-35; yet Satan was able to "fill" their hearts to lie to the Holy Spirit in Acts 5:3!

So we see that there is an abundance of Scriptural evidence for the possibility of a Christian having a demon. Furthermore, we are often exhorted to recognize and resist the attacks of the enemy.

In 2 Corinthians 11:3-4, Paul exhorts the believers at Corinth to remain true to the Gospel. He sets forth the possibility that they could, if they were not careful, "receive a different spirit" which was undoubtedly a spirit of error and deception (cf. Matt. 24:4; 2 Thess. 2:3; 1 John 3:7).

In 1 Timothy 4:1, Paul gives a strong admonition to the believers to guard themselves, in view of the fact that "in later times some will abandon the faith and follow deceiving spirits and things taught by demons."

In Galatians 3:1, Paul accuses the Christians in Galatia of having been "bewitched" by false teachers with their false doctrines.

All of these references reveal the possibility of a believer being seriously oppressed and influenced by Satan.

There are frequent exhortations in the New Testament that believers should resist the devil and his demons (e.g., Rom. 16:20; Jam. 4:7). If believers were automatically delivered and protected from Satan's influence and oppression, what sense could we make of Paul's command, in Ephesians 4:27, to "not give the devil a foothold"?

In 1 Peter 5:8, Peter exhorts the early believers to be sober and vigilant because their adversary "the devil prowls around like a roaring lion looking for someone to devour." This warning was not addressed to unbelievers – he wrote to Christian people. Satan is seeking to devour Spirit-filled Christians! In this passage, it is not a question of a believer having a demon, but it is the other way around: if the believer isn't vigilant, the demon may have him!

It is possible that God in His mercy may set an unbeliever free from demonic oppression, but the promise of deliverance is primarily for His people (Col. 1:13, Luke 10:19-20). In fact, Christians are the only people who can expect to be set free and remain free since expelled demons will return to see if their former habitation is still available (Matt. 12:44-45).

In summary, demons can be either inside or outside a believer. If they are inside, they should be cast out. If outside, they should be kept out.

THE QUESTION OF POSSESSION

As we have seen, demons look upon the person's life as their home (Matt. 12:43-45). But we must use the correct terminology to describe this. In reality, people are not "possessed" by demons; they "have" demons or are "demonized."

An exhaustive study of every relevant passage in the original Greek text of the New Testament yields the following terms that are used with regard to demons influencing people:

- A person can be demonized (Matt. 4:24).
- A person can have a demon (Mark 7:25).
- A person can be oppressed by a demon (Acts 10:38).
- A person can be vexed or troubled by a demon (Luke 6:18).
- A person can suffer or be afflicted by a demon (Matt. 17:15).
- A person can be "in" a demon, or under its influence (Mark 1:23).
- A person can have a demon "in" him (Acts 19:16).

But, in the New Testament, people are never said to be "possessed" by Satan or a demon. The most frequently used terms are to "have" a demon and to be "demonized." The King James term "possessed" is translated from the Greek word "daimonizomai." It is better translated "demonized" since the Greek word has no reference to ownership or property. Very few people are so given over to the control of demons that they could be described as "possessed" with demons. It is more accurate to say that people "have" demons, or that people are "demonized."

A demonized person is not completely controlled by demons. Usually only certain areas of a demonized person's life are affected. For example, a person's body may be well, but he is afflicted with depression. Another person may have peace in the daylight hours, but have a terrible fear of darkness. Satan has a measure of control in such a life, but not total control. Such a person is not "possessed" by demons in the sense that he is brimming over with nothing but demons, but there is an area of his life that is under the influence of demons. He is demonized in that area. A person can be demonized in one area of his life, and have liberty and peace in other areas.

In the account of Matt. 9:32, a dumb man with demons was brought to Jesus. He had a demon that made him unable to speak, but he was not totally possessed. His body was probably healthy and his mind clear, but he had a demon affecting him in the area of his speech. After the demon was cast out he could speak.

Much misunderstanding has resulted from the use of the word "possessed." This word suggests total ownership of a person by a demon, and on the basis of such Scriptures as 1 Corinthians 6:19-20, which says that our bodies and spirits belong to God, many Christians have rejected the idea that Christians can have demons, reasoning that a believer cannot be "possessed" by God and Satan at the same time.

However, when we realize that it is not a matter of "possession," the situation changes. Believers are not "possessed" by Satan, but they can "have demons" or be "demonized." They can be oppressed, harassed, and influenced by Satan without being "possessed" by him.

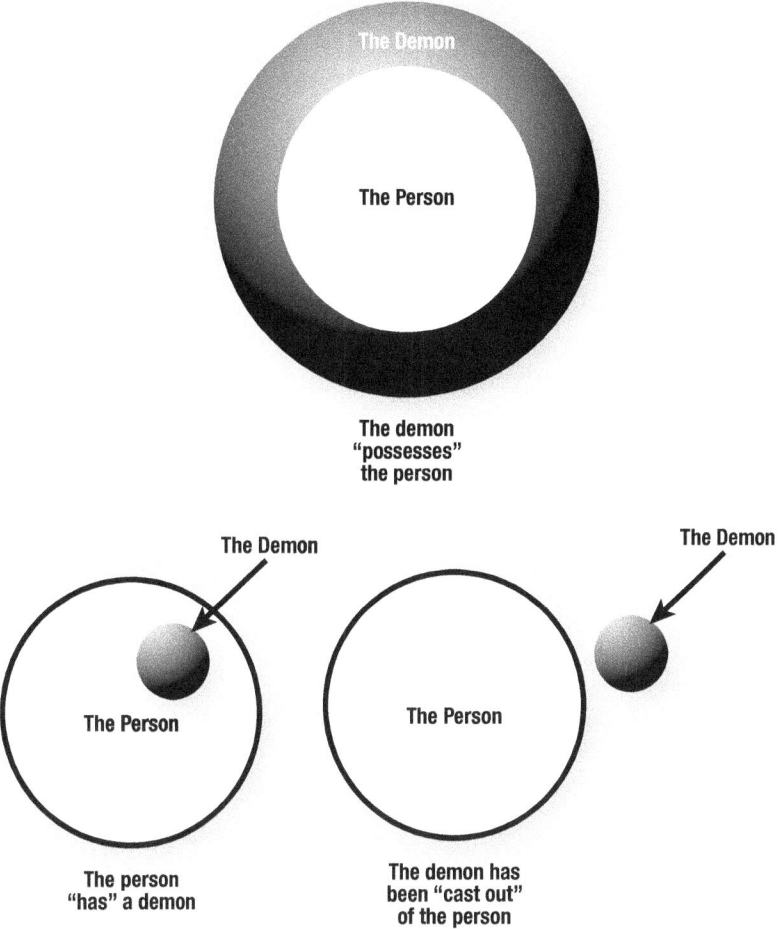

The various relationships between a demon and its "host" person are illustrated by the following graphics.

We need to get away from the idea that the only people who are bound by demons are mentally deranged madmen. Hollywood films such as "The Exorcist" have established this misconception in our culture.

But the fact is, people having demons is much more a normal part of life than we realize. As long as we think that the only people who have problems with demons are people who are deranged "possessed" people, we will continue to let Satan hide in our lives under the guise of personality flaws, habits, compulsions, fears, and so forth. Demons are highly skilled at hiding within personalities. Often we simply excuse ourselves:

> "Well, I'm just like that."
> "My father had a problem with anger, and so do I."
> "I've always had a problem with lust."

All the while, we really need deliverance. Thus, understanding and using the correct terminology unmasks the real question. It is not "is someone brimming over with nothing but demons?", but "is there an area of his life that is under the influence of demons?"

The valuable distinction is not whether someone is "possessed" or not, but rather: "Are the evil spirits on the outside or on the inside?" Do the demons have a hold on the person's life? The Chinese Christians describe this as a demon being "attached" to the believer. If the demons are on the inside (if they are "attached" to the believer) they need to be cast out in Jesus' name – their hold needs to be broken. If they're on the outside, they are simply to be resisted and kept out.

WORKS OF DEMONS OR WORKS OF THE FLESH?

> *For if you live according to the sinful nature, you will die; but if by the Spirit you put to death the misdeeds of the body, you will live, (Rom. 8:13)*

> *Since we have these promises, dear friends, let us purify ourselves from everything that contaminates body and spirit, perfecting holiness out of reverence for God. (2 Cor. 7:1)*

It is the responsibility of every Christian to yield to the working of the Holy Spirit and crucify the flesh. Every believer experiences areas of difficulty. If the problem is in your own heart, yield to God and surrender to the death of the cross. If you simply cannot overcome, then you probably have a demon that needs to be cast out. You cannot crucify a demon, but neither can you cast out the flesh. So start with crucifying the flesh, but if it doesn't work and you can't get the victory in that area of your life, then it may be a demon you're dealing with.

Symptoms of demonic oppression include compulsive behaviors, intrusive and ungodly thoughts, inability to control thoughts, hereditary patterns of illness, addiction or sin, inability to concentrate while praying and reading the Bible, constant depression or condemnation, unfounded fears, hatred of authority.

It is possible that some of these conditions may proceed from a lack of personal discipline, but frequently they indicate the presence and activity of demons. It is not always sin on the part of an oppressed Christian that opens the door to demons, but it is sin to keep the demon once the demon is exposed.

HOW DEMONS ENTER

Demons seek to carry out their missions of destruction in any individual's life, but barriers established by God prevent their indiscriminate entry. When these barriers are let down, however, demons will attach themselves to a part of the person or personality and remain there. This is why we are told to give no foothold to the devil (Eph. 4:27).

Demons gain entrance in a variety of ways, often referred to as "open doors." By recognizing these "doors," we can be on our guard to prevent their entry and also to close doors of entry in our lives and the lives of others through confession and repentance.

Demons can enter lives in the following ways:

- Through the family line. Evil spirits are frequently present in a person's life from before birth as a result of the sin of one of the parents or ancestors that opened a door. Often they will pass from parent to child and remain for generations in a family line (Ex. 20:5; 34:7; Num. 14:18; Deut. 5:9). Alcoholism, heart disease, rage, mental illness, and many other conditions affecting generations are often the result of demons passing from parent to child in that family. Through the principle of psychic heredity, witches and mediums often gain power with each successive generation as Satan's hold intensifies. (Note: the principle of generational increase also applies to believers. A believer with a godly heritage should expect to exceed the spiritual maturity and gifting of his parents as he builds upon their prayers and experiences.)

- Ignorance. Allowing occult objects in your home, listening to certain kinds of music, watching the wrong things on TV or movies, yielding to bizarre spiritual influences in a Christian meeting, giving yourself to unbridled emotionalism during times of stress, and many other similar activities can open a person to demonization.

  By not disciplining their children correctly, parents may unintentionally reinforce wrong behaviors that invite the oppression of demons in their children. For example, if parents allow their child to give himself over to temper tantrums when he doesn't get his own way, the child may open the door to demons of anger and rage.

- Traumatic experiences and emotional crises. Demons may take advantage of a crisis situation, when a person (without sinning) may be overwhelmed and allow spirits to enter. For example, a person who nearly drowns may open himself up to a spirit of fear because he did not react in faith or later deal with the trauma of that experience in prayer. A person attacked by a dog may open himself to a fear of dogs. A child who watches his drunken father beat his mother can open the door to demons of hatred, resentment, anger, fear, etc.

One boy who lost several family members when he was four years old opened the door to spirits of sadness and grief. He remained severely oppressed for many years until he was finally set free by the casting out of those spirits.

- Occult involvement. Occult refers to involvement in seeking or worshiping other gods. The Bible predicts a great increase in demonic activity in the last days.

  The Spirit clearly says that in later times some will abandon the faith and follow deceiving spirits and things taught by demons. (1 Tim. 4:1)

  This can be through cults (Mormons, Jehovah's Witnesses, etc.) and false religions (Hinduism, Buddhism, Shamanism, etc.), but also through more subtle ways. Satan does not come dressed up in red with horns and a pitchfork. He comes looking attractive, cool, inviting, and fun.

  …Satan himself masquerades as an angel of light. (2 Cor. 11:14)

  People are fascinated with the supernatural, so he easily draws them into a myriad of forbidden practices. Many of these things do give entrance into the supernatural or spiritual realm, but it is an entrance unauthorized by God. These practices are anything but harmless! A partial list includes witchcraft, casting spells, Satanism, fortune telling, tarot cards, aura reading, crystal balls, tea leaves, ouija board, role-playing games, séances, divination in various forms such as water witching and pendulums, hypnotism, astrology, horoscopes, reincarnation, reading occult books, yoga (relaxation states), eastern meditation, E.S.P., Freemasonry, mind reading, aromatherapy, hallucinogenic drugs, crystals and gems, spiritism, magic (black and white), palmistry, astral projection, hand writing analysis, iridology, occult healing (e.g., blowing off warts, acupuncture), telepathy, martial arts, table-tipping, levitation, automatic writing, dream interpretation, numerology, occult use of candles, occult use of magnets, occult use of herbs, rituals, occult-oriented rock music, voodoo, bestiality, making blood pacts, gang allegiances, and similar activities.

Occult objects and jewelry, pagan or religious symbols, images or idols, Amish hex symbols, charms, or decorations also allow entrance of demons. New converts in the city of Ephesus destroyed their valuable occult objects in order to sever all connections with the powers of darkness (Acts 19:18-19).

These and other such practices are condemned in many Scriptures:

> *When you enter the land the* LORD *your God is giving you, do not learn to imitate the detestable ways of the nations there. Let no one be found among you who sacrifices his son or daughter in the fire, who practices divination or sorcery, interprets omens, engages in witchcraft, or casts spells, or who is a medium or spiritist or who consults the dead. Anyone who does these things is detestable to the* LORD, *and because of these detestable practices the* LORD *your God will drive out those nations before you. You must be blameless before the* LORD *your God. The nations you will dispossess listen to those who practice sorcery or divination. But as for you, the* LORD *your God has not permitted you to do so. (Deut. 18:9-14)*

When a person participates in any form of occultism, whether deliberately, in ignorance, or merely out of curiosity, he violates the First Commandment and opens himself to demonic oppression.

The list of possible forms of oppression that result from occult and related sin is endless: lust, deceit, lying, pride, homosexuality, pornography, drug and alcohol addiction, gluttony, eating disorders, crime, arson, fear, worry, anxiety, disease, anger, violent temper, irresponsibility, hate, persistent illness, apathy, marital problems, rebellion against parents and authorities, insanity, self-pity, religious delusions, confusion, compulsive behavior, manic-depression, negativity, gloominess, emotional instability, spiritual indifference regarding worship or prayer or the Word, doubt, unbelief, resistance against God or His Word, apparitions, poltergeist activity (German for "noisy ghost"), voices, nightmares, sleeplessness, depression, suicide, etc.

And if that is not enough, the curses and open doors that stem from occult involvement affect not only the individual, but also his or her children and grandchildren in subsequent generations:

> *...I, the L*ORD *your God, am a jealous God, punishing the children for the sin of the fathers to the third and fourth generation of those who hate me, (Ex. 20:5)*

Curses relating to the occult are carried down through the bloodline. For this reason virtually everyone who comes to Christ carries with him guilt of occult sin that allows oppression to continue.

One other way that demons can enter is through curses or hexes that are cast by a person involved in magic of some kind. While the believer who is walking in the fear of God need not fear these (Ps. 121:6; Prov. 26:2), those that had been placed previously should be addressed in deliverance.

- Sin. According to Romans 6:16, when we yield to sin, we become slaves to sin. We open the door for demon powers to come and enslave us to the sin we gave ourselves to. Don't deliberately sin thinking that God will forgive you later. You are opening yourself up to potential oppression and affliction of many kinds. Deuteronomy 28:15-68 gives quite a list of the affliction and suffering that result from sin! Sin gives Satan a legal right in your life.

- Receiving wrong doctrine. Consider Paul's words to Timothy:

  And the Lord's servant must not quarrel; instead, he must be kind to everyone, able to teach, not resentful. Those who oppose him he must gently instruct, in the hope that God will grant them repentance leading them to a knowledge of the truth, and that they will come to their senses and escape from the trap of the devil, who has taken them captive to do his will. (2 Tim. 2:24-26)

  Clearly those who "follow deceiving spirits and things taught by demons" (1 Tim. 4:1; cf. 1 John 4:1-3) allow Satan significant place in their lives.

CASTING OUT DEMONS

Jesus cast out demons (Mark 1:39). The 12 cast out demons (Matt. 10:1). The 70 cast out demons (Luke 10:17). Moreover, all believers are to cast out demons (Mark 16:17).

Casting out demons is not a polite, gentle thing. We do not ask demons to "please leave." We are dealing with violent, aggressive, rebellious, stubborn spirit beings, who are trying to trespass in our lives. They are to be violently expelled with commands of faith. The Greek term used to express this is *ekballo*. Its forceful meaning is highlighted in its use in other contexts:

All the people in the synagogue were furious when they heard this. They got up, <u>drove</u> him out of the town, and took him to the brow of the hill on which the town was built, in order to throw him down the cliff. (Luke 4:28-29)

So he made a whip out of cords, and <u>drove</u> all from the temple area, both sheep and cattle; he scattered the coins of the money changers and overturned their tables. (John 2:15)

At this they covered their ears and, yelling at the top of their voices, they all rushed at him, <u>dragged</u> him out of the city and began to stone him. Meanwhile, the witnesses laid their clothes at the feet of a young man named Saul. (Acts 7:57-58)

We are to violently take the Kingdom (Matt. 11:12), and that includes casting out demons.

STUDY QUESTIONS

1. To what extent can demons influence a believer?
2. Why is the term "possession" not a good choice?
3. How should the believer deal with the works of the flesh? The works of a demon?
4. Why should occult objects be removed whenever possible?
5. Can occult involvement be harmless when the person is ignorant of the dangers?

Preparation for Deliverance

UNDERSTAND THE BELIEVER'S NEW LIFE IN CHRIST

God created man in His own image from the dust of the earth, and breathed into him the breath of life. Adam and Eve enjoyed continual fellowship with God in an environment free from sin, sickness and bondage. After their sin, death began to work in Adam and Eve, and was passed on to all their descendents. They were cut off from communion with God, their bodies began to experience the death process, and their spiritual lives became corrupt. The curse of sin touched every aspect of their lives and environment, and successive generations continued the downward spiral of sin and death.

> *Therefore, just as sin entered the world through one man, and death through sin, and in this way death came to all men, because all sinned (Rom. 5:12)*

The tragic state of mankind did not take God by surprise. The plan of redemption was in His heart from all eternity. In the fullness of time, God sent His Son into the world, born supernaturally of a virgin. Jesus lived as a man in perfect obedience to the will of God. He could then offer Himself as a substitutionary sacrifice for the sin of the world. Jesus bore the judgment of sin on our behalf. Through faith in Him, we are forgiven, released from the penalty and power of sin, and partake of His righteousness (Col. 2:15; 1 John 3:8; 2 Cor. 5:21). We identify with Jesus Christ by faith in His death, burial, and resurrection. Just as Jesus was raised by the power of God, we too are raised to newness of life in Him (Rom. 6). We can now say to the powers of darkness: "I have died to your power and I now live and reign as a child of God. I am seated in the heavenlies with Christ and I use my authority in Christ to overcome you. I declare myself free in Jesus' name." The Christian life is a life of victory over sin, rather than an endless cycle of sinning, asking forgiveness, and then sinning again. How do we transform this promise of victory into a day-to-day experience of victory? The answer is by faith.

WALK BY FAITH

The word faith comes from the Greek *pistos*. The related term "believe" is the verb *pisteo*, from the same root. Biblical faith is embracing the unseen spiritual reality revealed in God's Word. It is our connection to God, a medium of exchange through which we access the resources of heaven (Heb. 6:12). It is contrasted with works, yet it is revealed through our works (Rom. 3:28; Jam. 2:18). It is also contrasted with sight, yet its fruit can be seen (Heb. 11:3; Rom. 4:17). It is our link to the spiritual heritage of Abraham (Rom. 4:16), who because of his faith was justified and called a friend of God. Faith motivates and transforms our entire way of perceiving, thinking, and acting (Rom. 1:17; Acts 6:7; Rom. 15:18).

So central is faith to the life of the believer, that the term is used to embody all of Christian life and doctrine: "obedient to the faith" (Acts 6:7), "the household of faith" (Gal. 6:10), "one faith" (Eph. 4:5), "I have kept the faith" (2 Tim. 4:7). The passage from Habakkuk *"The just shall live by faith"* is quoted in the New Testament epistles. Since "without faith it is impossible to please God" (Heb. 11:6), it would certainly be impossible to live a life of victory without faith.

Faith is defined in Heb. 11:1 (NKJV): "Now faith is the substance of things hoped for, the evidence of things not seen." The terms "substance" and "evidence" are used to describe things that exist. The entire spiritual realm is more real than the realm of our senses and experience, and faith is the means by which we relate to this realm.

Faith is related to hope, but should not be confused with hope. Hope, which deals with the future, is a general expectation of good. Faith, however, deals with the present. Our hope is the catalyst for faith, but faith is what receives the promises.

Faith operates outside of the realm of our physical senses. Before the new birth, we were dead to God and unable to comprehend spiritual truth (1 Cor. 2:14). After the new birth, we are given a measure of faith and we can relate to the unseen realm of the spirit by faith. Everything God promises comes to us by virtue of Jesus' work at Calvary, and is received by grace through faith (Eph. 2:8). Redemption was fully accomplished, and now we apply it by faith. This includes our authority over oppressing spirits. Therefore, we can receive our deliverance by faith, then war *from* the position of victory rather than *for* the victory.

Faith comes through the Word of God (Rom. 10:17). God's Word is truth, and truth applied will make us free (John 8:32). Through the Word of God we learn about the character, power and faithfulness of God to lead and transform His people.

Choose passages of Scripture that relate to faith, what the death and resurrection of the Lord Jesus have done for you, and your particular area of need. Be sure to make daily time in the Word of God a priority. As you meditate on the truths of Scripture, you will find that the Holy Spirit, who is your Teacher (John 14:26), will cause the Word of God to take root in your heart and strengthen your faith. You may not see the difference from one day to the next, but over time, your trust in God to fulfill His promises will increase. As our faith is directed to God in prayer and obedience, God responds by bringing to pass the promises of His Word.

Instruction in the operation of faith is given in Mark 11:24:

Therefore I tell you, whatever you ask for in prayer, believe that you have received it, and it will be yours.

While this is not to be used as a "formula for success," there are three elements we can apply:

1. Pray and ask. Clearly it is God's will for His children to be free of demonic oppression since Jesus provided complete redemption at Calvary. Therefore, stand on the Word of God, and pray and ask for your complete deliverance once and for all.

2. Believe. Having asked for the provision, "believe that you have received it." Even if immediate change is not felt, the evidence of the provision is faith – faith that has come through the Word of God.

3. "It will be yours." Because you have already received the provision by faith, *"it will"* be granted in the realm of sight. Therefore you do not need to continue to ask for it, but rather thank God and praise Him for what is yours. Your faith is the evidence. The Holy Spirit will release into your experience what you received by faith when you prayed. This is the promise of God's Word. But often a period of time is involved, whether moments or months, or even years. God often allows a time of testing to strengthen character and reveal the genuineness of your faith. If you are merely following a formula, you will be disappointed, but if this truth is operating from your heart, you will receive the experience no matter how long the delay.

Understanding this faith principle as it relates to deliverance, you might pray something like this:

"Heavenly Father, I have asked many times that you would change me and deliver me, but now I see from Your Word that it is Your will for me to walk in the freedom of Calvary. Lord, I come to ask you one final time: Please deliver me from all bondages of the enemy. I ask in Jesus' name for this provision and I receive my deliverance now. I receive complete salvation for every part of me. By faith I receive total freedom. The bands of darkness are loosed! I am free! Thank You, Father, in Jesus' name."

Now you can battle Satan's demons, not *for* the victory, but *from* the place of victory.

> *We do not want you to become lazy, but to imitate those who through faith and patience inherit what has been promised. (Heb. 6:12)*

Name specific areas of bondage and declare that they are defeated. Command the spirits of darkness to leave in the name of Jesus, declaring that they now have no legal ground in your life. There is power in speaking to areas of bondage and commanding release in Jesus' name. Just as Jesus healed and delivered by His Word, we use our spiritual weapons through our words. In the passage in Mark 11, Jesus declared that we could move a mountain by faith. You may not be able to move mountains as quickly as Jesus could, but you can get the same results by removing them little by little. As you speak the word of faith to the demonic stronghold, you could imagine yourself moving the mountain with a bulldozer, or even a shovel. You don't have to feel full of power, because it is by faith that we overcome. The key is to believe that God will fulfill His promises when you confront demonic bondages, speaking in Jesus' name, and using the weapons of your warfare. Faith is now! This will weaken and break the enemy's hold. Slowly and surely your faith will flatten any mountain of oppression (Is. 41:15-16).

KNOW YOUR WEAPONS

God has given the believer "all things that pertain to life and godliness" (2 Pet. 1:3). This includes all the equipping necessary to obtain the freedom from bondage to the powers of darkness, that Jesus provided through His death and resurrection. The full armor of God described in

Ephesians 6:14-18 is ours as we "put on Christ" (Rom. 13:12-14). Jesus is truth, the righteousness of God, our peace, the source of our faith, our Salvation, and the Living Word. As we acknowledge Him daily as our life and strength, we are more than conquerors. Along with the armor of God, we have spiritual weapons that are more than adequate to meet the onslaughts of the powers of darkness.

> *The weapons we fight with are not the weapons of the world. On the contrary, they have divine power to demolish strongholds. (2 Cor. 10:4)*

God has given us many powerful weapons to use in our battles with the forces of darkness. We do not have to use all the weapons in every battle, but we must be knowledgeable of each of them. These weapons are used by faith and they include:

1. The Name of Jesus.

Jesus said of believers: "In my name they will drive out demons" (Mark 16:17). The gospels and Book of Acts contain many miracles of healing and deliverance done by ordinary people through Jesus' mighty name. This is because the name of Jesus represents the presence and power of Jesus Himself when we use it as His representatives on earth.

> *The seventy-two returned with joy and said, "Lord, even the demons submit to us in your name." (Luke 10:17)*

> *By faith in the name of Jesus, this man whom you see and know was made strong. It is Jesus' name and the faith that comes through him that has given this complete healing to him, as you can all see. (Acts 3:16; cf. v. 12)*

> *...Paul became so troubled that he turned around and said to the spirit, "In the name of Jesus Christ I command you to come out of her!" At that moment the spirit left her. (Acts 16:18)*

> *Therefore God exalted him to the highest place and gave him the name that is above every name, that at the name of Jesus every knee should bow, in heaven and on earth and under the earth, and every tongue confess that Jesus Christ is Lord, to the glory of God the Father. (Phil. 2:9-11)*

2. **The Word of God.**

Jesus gave us an example of victory through the Word of God when he overcame each temptation of the devil with Scripture (Luke 4:4, 8, 12). The Word of God is truth, and the enemy is subject to it.

The truth of the Word of God is also needed to pull down strongholds behind which the enemy hides. This is usually some lie or deception. For example, a spirit of rejection may hide behind a particular wrong thought pattern such as "I'm ugly and worthless." As our minds are renewed by the Word, these lies will be exposed and replaced by God's truth, such as "I am accepted in the beloved. I am valuable because Jesus shed His blood for me."

If someone has been bound by fear, he can be encouraged and set free by the power of God's truth:

> *For God has not given us a spirit of fear, but of power and of love and of a sound mind. (2 Tim. 1:7, NKJV)*

We must also learn to recognize the word that God speaks to our hearts by His Spirit. Just as Jesus was led by the Spirit in how He prayed and ministered, we must obey the Holy Spirit as He brings the truth of His Word to our minds.

One area of truth that is of particular importance is our identification with Jesus' death, burial, and resurrection. The entire sixth chapter of Romans needs to be read and meditated upon, because our victory over Satan is actually Christ's victory that we share.

This is very powerful.

For example, if we have been greatly rejected in our life, and spirits of rejection have found a place, one of the keys to release is to say what we have become in Christ according to His Word: "Spirits of rejection, you have no right to affect me. I have died to this world, and to your dominion. I have died to the feelings of hurt and rejection you bring. Rejection, your power is broken. I am now alive in Christ. His power has set me free and His love fills my innermost being. Thank you, God, that these spirits are leaving me right now. This stronghold is crumbling and every band is broken, in Jesus' name."

Some Scriptures to meditate on and memorize are:

- Is. 53:5 – I am healed of all physical diseases in Him.
- John 6:56 – I live in Christ and Christ lives in me.
- John 15:16 – I am appointed to go and bear fruit.
- Acts 1:8 – I am endued with power by the Holy Spirit.
- Rom. 3:24 – I am justified freely by God's grace in Christ.
- Rom. 8:1 – I am free from condemnation.
- Rom. 8:2 – I am free from the law of sin and death.
- Rom. 8:16-17 – I am a child of God, an heir of God, and joint-heir with Christ.
- Rom. 8:37 – I am more than a conqueror.
- Rom. 8:39 – Nothing can separate me from God's love.
- 1 Cor. 1:2 – I am set apart in Christ.
- 1 Cor. 1:30 – I have wisdom, righteousness, sanctification and redemption in Christ.
- 2 Cor. 1:21 – I stand firm in Christ.
- 2 Cor. 2:14 – God always causes me to triumph in Christ.
- 2 Cor. 3:5-6 – I am an able minister of the New Covenant.
- 2 Cor. 3:14 – Every barrier between me and God is removed in Christ.
- 2 Cor. 5:17 – I am a new creation in Christ.
- 2 Cor. 5:20 – I am an ambassador for Jesus Christ.

- 2 Cor. 5:21 – I am the righteousness of God in Christ.
- Gal. 2:4 – I have liberty in Christ.
- Eph. 1:3 – I am blessed with every spiritual blessing in the heavenlies.
- Eph. 1:4 – I was chosen in Christ before the foundation of the world.
- Eph. 1:6 – I am accepted in Christ.
- Eph. 2:6 – I am seated with Christ in the heavenlies.
- Eph. 2:10 – I am His workmanship.
- Col. 1:13-14 – I am delivered from Satan's dominion.
- Col. 2:10 – I am complete in Him.
- 2 Tim. 1:9 – I have divine purpose and the grace to fulfill that purpose.
- 1 Pet. 5:14 – I have peace in Christ.

Through the Word of God we have victory over the powers of darkness. Therefore, we must know the Word:

Do not let this Book of the Law depart from your mouth; meditate on it day and night, so that you may be careful to do everything written in it. Then you will be prosperous and successful. (Josh. 1:8)

Then you will know the truth, and the truth will set you free. (John 8:32)

3. The Blood of Jesus.

As God instructed the Hebrews in Egypt to place the blood of the Passover lamb on the door posts of their home with the promise that the destroyer would not be allowed to enter (Ex. 12), so we can by faith put the blood of Jesus over our lives and families.

They overcame him by the blood of the Lamb and by the word of their testimony; they did not love their lives so much as to shrink from death. (Rev. 12:11)

Testify to what the Word says the blood has accomplished. Demons hate to hear the following words:

- I am cleansed from all sin by the blood of Jesus (1 John 1:7).
- I am brought near to God by the blood of Jesus (Eph. 2:13).
- I am justified by the blood of Jesus (Rom. 5:8-9).
- I have redemption by the blood of Jesus (Eph. 1:7).
- I am sanctified by the blood of Jesus (Heb. 13:12).
- I have peace with God by the blood of Jesus (Col. 1:20).
- I am in a covenant relationship with God by the blood of Jesus (Mark 14:24).
- I am purchased by the blood of Jesus (Acts 20:28).
- The blood of Jesus cleanses my conscience (Heb. 9:14).
- I have confidence to come into the presence of God by the blood of Jesus (Heb. 10:19-22).
- The blood of Jesus is precious to me (1 Pet. 1:19).

Demons hate the mention of the blood of Jesus because it reminds them of their defeat at the cross (Col. 2:14-15; Heb. 2:14).

4. The Holy Spirit.

The Holy Spirit is the One who reveals Jesus in our midst (John 14:18). He is the one who strengthens us for the battle, who quickens the words we utter in faith in Jesus' name. By His power we are enabled to cast out demons.

> *But if I drive out demons by the Spirit of God, then the kingdom of God has come upon you. (Matt. 12:28)*

> *how God anointed Jesus of Nazareth with the Holy Spirit and power, and how he went around doing good and healing all who were under the power of the devil, because God was with him. (Acts 10:38)*

Jesus did not begin His ministry until He was anointed with the Holy Spirit. He did not cast out a single demon or work a single healing or miracle until He had received the Spirit's anointing. Therefore, our ministry to ourselves and others will not be effective apart from the Holy Spirit in our lives. The baptism in the Holy Spirit is not an end in itself, but it is a gateway through which we enter into a greater realm of power and service to God. Without this experience we will never successfully and consistently deal with evil spirits. We must have the baptism in the Holy Spirit!

> *But you will receive power when the Holy Spirit comes on you; and you will be my witnesses in Jerusalem, and in all Judea and Samaria, and to the ends of the earth. (Acts 1:8)*

> *If you then, though you are evil, know how to give good gifts to your children, how much more will your Father in heaven give the Holy Spirit to those who ask him! (Luke 11:13)*

You may receive the baptism in the Holy Spirit either by the laying on of hands or through your own personal prayer of faith. You do not need to beg or plead with God to receive the Holy Spirit. Neither do you need to "tarry" or wait for the Holy Spirit inasmuch as He has already been poured out upon the church. You need simply to ask God once to baptize you, and He will.

You do not necessarily need someone else to help you receive the Holy Spirit. If you are alone, you can pray right now and ask Him to come and fill you. The following are simple and effective steps to take to receive the baptism in the Holy Spirit:

a) Believe that it is God's will to give you the Holy Spirit on the basis of His promises in His Word:

> *If you then, though you are evil, know how to give good gifts to your children, how much more will your Father in heaven give the Holy Spirit to those who ask him! (Luke 11:13)*

> *Peter replied, "Repent and be baptized, every one of you, in the name of Jesus Christ for the forgiveness of your sins. And you will receive the gift of the Holy Spirit. The promise is for you and your children and for all who are far off – for all whom the Lord our God will call." (Acts 2:38-39)*

b) Jesus said that God will give the Holy Spirit to "those who ask Him" (Luke 11:13). The reason why so many Christians do not have the baptism is simply because they have never asked in a definite manner expecting to receive the Holy Spirit with the sign of new tongues. Therefore, ask God for the Holy Spirit and believe Jesus' words when He said, "everyone who asks receives" (Luke 11:9-13).

c) Believe and acknowledge that you have received the Holy Spirit when you pray (Mark 11:24; 1 John 5:14-15).

For example, pray: "Father, in the name of Jesus, on the basis of your promise in your Word, I now ask you to fill me with your Holy Spirit. And, I thank you that because I have asked, I have right now received the Holy Spirit. I have been filled with the Holy Spirit, and I can now speak in new tongues. In Jesus' name. Amen."

d) Begin to speak in new tongues. Acts 2:4 says, "**they**...began to speak with other tongues, as the Spirit gave them utterance" (KJV). **You** must begin to speak. Simply begin to speak, except do not speak in English (as you cannot speak in two languages at once).

As you begin to speak, the Holy Spirit will give you utterance in a new language. Do not be concerned about "what to say," but simply begin to speak and the Holy Spirit will give you the words. As you begin to speak, you will find that you are speaking in a new language.

People do not always experience a great "feeling," "anointing," or "emotion" when they receive the baptism. It does not matter whether you do or not. Jesus said that your heavenly Father will give you the Holy Spirit when you ask, and He cannot lie. Therefore, simply thank God that He has filled you with the Holy Spirit and begin to speak in new tongues. Then continue to pray in tongues daily (Rom. 8: 26-27; 1 Cor. 14:2, 4, 5, 14-15, 18, 39; Eph. 6:18; Jude 20-21).

5. Speaking in Tongues.

The prayer language of the Holy Spirit is another way the Spirit equips us for battle. There are two aspects of speaking in tongues described in the New Testament. One aspect is the gift of tongues through which a believer gives a message to the church inspired by the Holy Spirit. This message must be accompanied by the gift of interpretation of tongues in order to benefit the church. The second aspect is prayer in the Holy Spirit, or praying in tongues, and is what we are dealing with here. On the day of Pentecost when the disciples were filled with the Holy Spirit, those nearby heard them speaking the praises of God in their own diverse languages, or tongues. This is the outward evidence of the baptism in the Holy Spirit that continues throughout the church age (Acts 2:38). Paul knew the blessing of using this unlearned language inspired by the Holy Spirit and said to the saints in Corinth, "I thank God that I speak in tongues more than all of you." (1 Cor. 14:18). Through praying in tongues, which is something the believer can do any time he wants to, the believer builds himself up (1 Cor. 14:4). A believer confronting demonic powers in his life will need the strength that the Holy Spirit imparts through speaking in tongues.

In the process of deliverance, praying in tongues is effective because it is praying the perfect will of God (Rom. 8:26-27). The Holy Spirit knows how to pray for deep needs that we may not have the understanding to pray for. In addition, when praying for others to be set free, commanding in tongues as the Spirit leads may bring about the breakthrough.

6. **The Gifts of the Spirit.**

The Holy Spirit is also the source of the spiritual gifts. The gift of discerning of spirits is one of the nine gifts listed in 1 Corinthians 12:9-11. Through this gift, the believer's eyes are opened to see or perceive things in the unseen realm that could not be perceived by natural knowledge or sight. While any believer may manifest spiritual discernment on occasion, some have received this gift from the Holy Spirit and operate in it consistently.

As with any gift of the Holy Spirit, it should be used to edify the body of Christ and promote the kingdom of God. Obviously a person with the gift of discernment of spirits would be a valuable asset for a deliverance ministry team. The gifts of faith, working of miracles, and word of knowledge are also greatly beneficial in a deliverance setting.[2]

7. **Laying On of Hands.**

The power of the Holy Spirit can be imparted through the laying on of hands. Jesus often laid His hands on people as He ministered (Luke 4:40-41), and He commissioned His disciples to do the same (Mark 16:18). Demons in people may react when hands are laid on their victims by attempting to push the hands away. Sometimes people feel heat or fire flowing as hands are laid on them.

Hands can be laid on the head or elsewhere, depending on the situation. A man praying for a man, or a woman praying for a woman may place a hand on the abdominal area since the deepest releases sometimes come from this region. However, when praying for someone of the opposite gender, care must be taken to avoid any appearance of evil.

---

[2] For a complete discussion of the gifts of the Holy Spirit, please see Strategic Press' book on this subject.

A man praying for a woman's deliverance should not lay hands on any part of her body except her head or shoulder. He should also have a woman working with him on the deliverance team. A woman praying for a man should take the same precautions.

Since the laying on of hands can be used for impartation, it is important to realize that it is possible to receive something that is not from the Holy Spirit. We must be selective as to who is laying their hands on us. A self-proclaimed minister that is filled with pride, for example, is not the one you want to lay hands on you! All believers should be in a place where they can lay hands on another and impart blessing, but sadly, this is not always the case.

On the other hand, it is not necessary for a believer who is walking in the light of God's Word with an honest and humble heart to be perfect or even completely free to pray for others and be used to minister healing and deliverance to others. If perfection were a prerequisite, no one would be ministering.

8. **Praise.**

This is a powerful weapon against Satan's works. The account in 2 Chronicles 20 describes how praise brought about the overthrow of the enemies of God's people in the days of Jehoshaphat:

> *After consulting the people, Jehoshaphat appointed men to sing to the LORD and to praise him for the splendor of his holiness as they went out at the head of the army, saying: "Give thanks to the LORD, for his love endures forever." As they began to sing and praise, the LORD set ambushes against the men of Ammon and Moab and Mount Seir who were invading Judah, and they were defeated. (vv. 21-22)*

This is true today. When battling unseen spirits, we should mingle our commands with praise to God, for our victory is in Him. God inhabits the praises of His people (Ps. 22:3).

The experience of Paul and Silas demonstrates the power of praise:

> *About midnight Paul and Silas were praying and singing hymns to God, and the other prisoners were listening to them. Suddenly there was such a violent earthquake that the foundations of the prison were shaken. At once all the prison doors flew open, and everybody's chains came loose. (Acts 16:25-26)*

One deliverance minister shared his experience in Papua New Guinea. At the close of a teaching, he led the people in a time of praise, expecting to end the meeting that way. Several young men began to break out in an enthusiastic heart-felt praise that quickly spread across the congregation as "high praise" (Psalm 149:6-9). The presence of God became so intense that dramatic deliverances began to take place. Demons were leaving with loud cries as the praises of God arose. This continued for about twenty minutes. After the meeting ended, those who did not receive full freedom remained for individual prayer. The demonic manifestations were violent, but the Holy Spirit fell again with the same intensity, as counselors rushed from person to person commanding release in Jesus' name. What a victory! The Holy Spirit came in power in response to faith and genuine praise.

9. **Anointed music.**

Anointed music can also bring the power of the Holy Spirit. Elisha called for a minstrel when the king of Israel sought his counsel concerning their enemies (2 Kings 3:15). Young David played his harp to drive away the spirit that tormented King Saul (1 Sam. 16:23). When you are in the presence of the Lord breaking areas of bondage, there may be times when music playing quietly in the background will strengthen and refresh you while compelling the enemy to leave.

10. **The spoken word.**

   > *When evening came, many who were demon-possessed were brought to him, and he drove out the spirits with a word...* (Matt. 8:16)

   Of course, when we do this, our words must be spoken "in Jesus' name" and not in our own authority.

   In the context of casting out demons, Jesus asked, "How can anyone enter a strong man's house and carry off his possessions unless he first ties up the strong man?" (Matt. 12:27-29). We "tie up" the enemy by casting him out with our words of faith (cf. v. 28). This releases those he has held captive.

   Satan was already disarmed through the death and resurrection of the Lord Jesus (Col. 2:15) so he must obey our words. As the enemy is cast out, God's people are set free.

11. **Fasting.**

   While there is no specific command in the New Testament to fast, there are passages that reveal fasting to be a normal part of the Christian life (Matt. 9:14-15). In the Sermon on the Mount, Jesus assumes His followers will fast and urges them to fast with the proper motives (Matt. 6:16-18). Fasting is an expression of the intensity of our hunger for God. Amidst the discomfort of our flesh, our inner man is strengthened and more yielded to the Holy Spirit.

   Sometimes a period of fasting, whether long or short, can greatly assist in breaking demonic strongholds. Fasting prepares the ground for the battle. When the disciples were not able to cast out a spirit, Jesus replied "This kind can come out by nothing but prayer and fasting" (Mark. 9:29, NKJV).

STUDY QUESTIONS

1. Why is faith necessary for freedom from demonic bondage?
2. Describe the importance of Scripture in defeating the work of demons. Give three examples from the Bible.
3. Why does the Cross mean defeat for the devil?
4. How did Jesus model ministry by the power of the Holy Spirit?

Setting Yourself Free

Self-deliverance is simply applying our authority over the powers of darkness to spirits in ourselves, using the spiritual weapons just described. The path to deliverance is very simple:

1. Receive salvation and the baptism in the Holy Spirit.
2. Repent generally from all sins, including the sins of previous generations.
3. Repent and renounce specific sins in areas of your life that you know are bound. Repentance breaks Satan's power to oppress you. Repentance is the key to deliverance.
4. Cast Satan out in Jesus' name.
5. Destroy any objects related to Satan's oppression.
6. Fulfill your ongoing responsibilities as a believer. Thus, you will maintain your freedom.

1. **Salvation and the baptism in the Holy Spirit.**

    The first step in obtaining freedom is to yield yourself by faith to the lordship of Jesus Christ and receive forgiveness of sins and eternal life. This is when deliverance begins. If you are not sure how to come to God, you can pray from your heart something like this:

    "Dear God, I confess that I have sinned against You, and I ask You now to forgive me. I turn from sin and from my own way. I have counted the cost of following Your Son, and I am willing to follow Him with my whole heart. I believe that Jesus Christ died for me and rose from the dead on the third day, having overcome the power of sin and Satan for me. I yield myself now to the lordship of Jesus. I give you my life. By faith, I receive forgiveness of sins and the gift of eternal life. Thank You, Lord Jesus, for saving me and for coming into my life. I will serve you forever. In the name of Jesus. Amen."

One of the first acts of obedience to Jesus will be water baptism, through which you publicly acknowledge your severance from the dominion of self, sin and Satan (Mark 16:16, Rom. 6). You will also need to ask the Lord Jesus to fill you with the Holy Spirit that you might live the Christian life with His power and enabling.

Now you are ready to address your areas of bondage and the spirits behind them in the following steps.

2. **Acknowledge areas of need and repent of related sins.**

Include all areas of occult sin through past generations in a general prayer of confession, and then include all specific sins that you are aware of – before and after you were saved. Keep in mind that repentance is a turning away from sin, not just an admission of sin. Put these under the blood of Jesus by faith.

Dear Heavenly Father, I acknowledge your lordship over my life. I ask for your protection and guidance as I use the authority Jesus has given me to set myself free from all the powers of darkness. I ask you to bring to my mind anything and everything I have done knowingly or unknowingly that involves any occult practice or anything that opened the door to demonic bondage. I confess that I have participated in .... [name specific sins and open doors]. I know now that it was wrong and I repent of it all and place it under the blood of Jesus. Thank you for your forgiveness, in Jesus' name.

3. **Renounce all ties to the enemy and his works in your life.**

Let the devil know that you belong to Jesus Christ and will no longer have any association with evil. If you are aware of specific ties to bondage, break each one by faith. For example, a parent may exert an unnatural control over an adult child that keeps him from moving on in his own life. This bondage of control should be broken while maintaining a loving attitude toward the offending parent. Any association to a false religion or anything that demands the allegiance that belongs to Jesus (e.g., a gang, a cult, or even a church) must be renounced.

(A spoken declaration) *I renounce .... [specific areas]. I close all doors including hereditary open doors on both sides of my family. I break all ties of bondage to .... [name individuals or sources]. I take back all ground that the enemy has gained in my life through the name and blood of the Lord Jesus Christ.*

4. **Command the demon spirits to leave in the name of Jesus.**

Attack the enemy confidently. Colossians 2:9-15 assures the believer that Satan is defeated through the cross of Christ. The hidden spirits you are attacking are defeated ones, because the price for your redemption has been paid in full. Your attack is on the grounds of Calvary's provision. Because you know your authority as a believer submitted to the Lord Jesus, and you are equipped with spiritual weapons and the armor of God, you can speak boldly to the enemy.

You might say, "In the name of the Lord Jesus Christ, I come against you hidden spirits and I break your power in my life. You can no longer hide because I now recognize what you have been doing. I renounce you and your works." Then speak to specific areas of need such as fear: "Spirits of fear, I speak directly to you. I drive you out of my life now. The blood of Jesus Christ has redeemed me. You have no legal right to touch me. You are leaving me now in the name of Jesus. Come up and out now. I cast you out now. By the power of the Holy Spirit I am free. Thank You, Lord Jesus, that You are taking my commands and making them as shafts of light against the darkness. I am free by the power of the blood of Jesus…"

As you pray, be sensitive to the Holy Spirit. He can bring things to your memory that will reveal the nature and origin of the bondage. Use this information in your warfare. For example, you may remember the day you were left alone in your house as a young child, and how from that time you began to experience abnormal fear. As this comes to your mind, you can be more specific with your commands: "I continue to speak against all fear. Every root of fear that gripped me when I was left alone as a child, I address you, and command you to leave in Jesus' name." As you speak, believe that what you say is happening. Use your sanctified imagination to picture what is happening as you release yourself. The Scriptures use figures such as bands, fetters, snares, strongholds, and yokes. Apply these pictures to the spiritual realm as you speak: "I break every chain of fear in the name of Jesus."

These commands should be spoken, but there is no need to shout. The demons respond to the anointing of the Holy Spirit, not noise. Address the devil through outward commands as well as inward ones.

If you experience a pressure, but you don't know the name of the spirit or spirits that are manifesting in this way, you can say something like: "I come against the source of this pressure. Every kind of spirit pressing me now, I am speaking to you. Go in Jesus' name."

Claim by faith your complete freedom in each area, then believe you have received. Determine that from this day forward, the time of continually asking is over, and the time of "taking the land" has begun. You may not have enough faith to remove an entire mountain with one command, but anyone can believe that a measure of weakening and breaking is taking place. "I stand against this stronghold of fear in the name of Jesus. Every kind of fear, your power is broken by the blood of Jesus. You have no place in my life. I overcome you by the blood of Jesus and the word of my testimony. I now expel you. Come out in Jesus' name. You are leaving me now. Thank You, Jesus, for the release I am receiving."

5. **Rid your home of objects that relate to the occult or areas of bondage. If you have not already done so, destroy all objects that give place to the devil.**

> *A number who had practiced sorcery brought their scrolls together and burned them publicly. When they calculated the value of the scrolls, the total came to fifty thousand drachmas. (Acts 19:19)*

This could include demonic music CD's, art objects such as a Buddha statue or some other religious image, occult books, horror videos, etc. Do not let the cost of these items stop you. The freedom you will experience is worth much more!

6. **Maintain your deliverance.**

> *When an evil spirit comes out of a man, it goes through arid places seeking rest and does not find it. Then it says, "I will return to the house I left." When it arrives, it finds the house unoccupied, swept clean and put in order. Then it goes and takes with it seven other spirits more wicked than itself, and they go in and live there. And the final condition of that man is worse than the first... (Matthew 12:43-45)*

This is a serious warning. Deliverance is a way of life, not an isolated event. Keeping the doors closed to the enemy requires a consistent and faithful Christian walk. If you follow the basic principle of submitting to God and resisting the devil (James 4:7), you can be confident that your freedom will be maintained.

Stay in the Word of God. Continue in faith, deliberately acknowledging the lordship of Jesus over every area of your life and regularly reading and meditating on God's Word. In particular, meditate upon the truth of your identification with Jesus Christ as outlined earlier. The way to success – full deliverance in this case –is identified in Joshua 1:8 as meditating on the Word of God continually and obeying from the heart. As you meditate on the Word of God it will cleanse and renew your mind (Rom. 12:2; Eph. 4:21-24).

Continue in prayer. Prayer is one of the ways we maintain our relationship with God and keep our hearts open to receive spiritual life and strength. Our Father invites us to come to Him with praise and thanksgiving and to cast all our cares upon Him. Included in this is praying in tongues. Jude 20 tells us that the believer builds himself up through praying in the Holy Spirit. Just as the Holy Spirit was the agent of your deliverance, He is also the agent through whom deliverance is maintained. Do not neglect praying in tongues – it is a great source of spiritual strength.

Be a functioning part of a local fellowship of believers that teaches the Bible, submits to the lordship of Jesus Christ, and honors the Holy Spirit. Don't be a spectator, but find your place of ministry and begin helping others. Isolated Christians remain easy targets for the enemy. As you get involved in the ministry of the body of Christ and serve others, you will avoid the snares of self-absorption. Ask for the prayers and support of your brothers and sisters as needed. Be sure to pray for them as well.

Resist the devil. Fill in the void (Matt. 12:44). Spirits can only return and bring others with them if the house is left vacant. As you are set free, consciously yield the newly freed areas to the Holy Spirit's control. Demon spirits will check on their former house, hoping to return. This may come in the form of temptation in the thought realm to sin or react in the area of previous oppression. These, of course, must be met with the Word of God and resisted.

Guard your mind. Be alert to the enemy's tactics of intimidation, temptation and deception. Do not allow the old thought patterns to reestablish themselves. Resist the devil. If you need help, ask other believers to pray with you.

Many Christians will feel condemned if there is a continuation or reoccurrence of a problem after deliverance, thinking they have given opportunity for spirits to return However, it is a mistake to think a lapse or setback is necessarily an indication of failure. This is often not the case. Rather what is often happening is that further spirits in the same area of bondage are stirring. Even though a major release has been experienced, there may still be many other spirits that need to come out. Continue to command release. See yourself as moving forward, not backward, becoming freer and not more bound. Through your faith and the ministry of the Holy Spirit, spirits within are being stirred up: you can become aware of them and drive them out. They feel the pressure, and that's why you feel it too.

So if a lapse occurs, deal with the sin quickly. Continuing in sin gives legal ground for evil spirits to enter. A Christian breaking through the bondage of the enemy cannot afford to be careless with sin or to grieve the Holy Spirit. Further, be alert to the enemy's tactics and avoid becoming ensnared through temptation. For example, a Christian delivered from spirits relating to sexual sins must stay clear of sights (magazines, internet pornography, etc.) and places where lust is exalted.

Your deliverance may be a process that begins at a specific time but extends through a period of days, weeks, or months until you are completely free. A strong area of bondage may involve many spirits and may require time. Spend time regularly in spiritual warfare until you come into freedom. Don't allow the devil to persuade you that you are spending too much time on deliverance. He will tell you anything that will hinder you from coming into freedom.

Realize that God is doing a good work in you through your struggles. As you persist in breaking bondages, you are becoming stronger and more like Jesus, as well as more free. Let this encourage you to press on when you feel weary from the battle.

STUDY QUESTIONS

1. How does repentance break the power of the enemy?
2. Should a believer address Satan directly? Why or why not?
3. How does the believer know when the demon has left?
4. What should be done if breakthrough is not immediate?
5. Why is the period of time following deliverance important?

Praying for Others to Be Set Free

RESPONSIBILITIES OF THE DELIVERANCE MINISTER

Helping others receive deliverance is a serious undertaking and requires preparation on the part of both the seeker and the one ministering deliverance. The minister should be consistently in fellowship with the Lord Jesus and regularly exercising spiritual disciplines such as fasting, prayer, and time in the Word of God. He must be willing to maintain confidentiality as the seeker shares details of his life that relate to his need. He should always seek to work within the structure of divinely appointed authority when ministering to women or youth.

It is strongly recommended that the minister be part of a deliverance team of perhaps three to five people for support and accountability. A minister will be benefited by the presence of helpers praying and supporting with the gifts of word of knowledge and discerning of spirits. Those who minister in deliverance are dealing directly with the powers of darkness and attempts at retaliation are best defended against by remaining teachable, humble, and accountable in a group setting.

RESPONSIBILITIES OF THE DELIVERANCE CANDIDATE

The seeker should be aware of his responsibility to resist the enemy before, during, and after deliverance. First and foremost, he must actually desire to be set free and be willing to pay the cost to obtain and maintain his deliverance. This may include giving up affection for a besetting sin, forgiving an offender, restitution, reconciliation, and removal or destruction of personal items connected with the occult and other sins. He must be willing, if necessary, to share freely his oppressions and their causes. He must be ready to follow through by establishing himself in the disciplines of the Word of God and prayer. He must be prepared to submit himself to the life of a local church. A prayer partner or group to whom he may be accountable can provide follow up support and encouragement.

PRELIMINARY DISCOURSE

A preliminary counseling session can be helpful. The minister can determine whether deliverance is needed and truly desired. Be sure that the conditions for a successful deliverance are met, such as willingness to forgive offenders, replace wrong thought patterns with the truth of the Word of God, etc. With that established, the nature of the bondage as well as probable causes (open doors) can be ascertained through discussion with the seeker.

THE DELIVERANCE

The next step is the actual deliverance. Begin with prayer for the presence, wisdom, and gifts of the Holy Spirit. You may also command that spirits about to be cast out receive no help or reinforcement from outside sources. There are diversities of operations and methods, but key ingredients in any deliverance will be:

1. Make sure the person involved is saved and filled with the Holy Spirit and truly wants freedom and is willing to continue resisting the enemy after the deliverance session.
2. Repentance of the deliverance candidate.
3. Closing of open doors.
4. Commands of faith directed at specific demons to immediately leave and not return.
5. Instruction in follow up (destroying occult objects, maintaining deliverance, etc.).

WHAT ABOUT MANIFESTATIONS?

Manifestations of demons should not be considered routine or to be expected. However, during deliverance, demons might at times speak through people, expressing their nature, their hatred of Christians, or attempting to intimidate a deliverance minister through vile threats. Since demons are liars, it is much better to know the Word of God and listen to the Holy Spirit than to try to gain information from prolonged discussions with demons. Occasionally it is necessary to command the demon to name itself, as Jesus did in Mark 9:9.

In the ministry of Jesus, demonic manifestations included speaking, crying out, throwing down and convulsing. Sometimes the manifestations were quite dramatic:

> *The spirit shrieked, convulsed him violently and came out. The boy looked so much like a corpse that many said, "He's dead." (Mark 9:26)*

Notably, the demons did not always instantly obey Jesus' command (e.g., Luke 8:29). If Jesus and the apostles (e.g., Acts 8:7) were not able to obtain instant deliverance without any physical manifestations, how should we expect to be able to do so?

Any manifestations, however bizarre, should be seen as merely the desperation of a defeated enemy and should not cause retreat or fear in those ministering in faith.

The exit of demons may be indicated by certain physical manifestations. These may include yawning, sighing, or even vomiting. Manifestations may or may not be visible during deliverance, so don't let your faith waver from the Great Deliverer and His promise to set His people free.

HINDRANCES TO DELIVERANCE

What if all the above principles are applied, yet deliverance does not occur? If the devil has legal ground on which to stand, he will not go. Here are a number of conditions that will give the enemy grounds to remain.

Unwillingness to repent. Repentance signifies a change of mind and direction. It demonstrates a heart of humility and submission to God. Repentance may be accompanied by feelings of remorse, but often it begins as a decision in response to the conviction of the Holy Spirit. It is a choice that we make by faith, knowing that the Holy Spirit will empower us to walk it out. Through repentance, darkness is exposed and renounced. Without willingness to repent, demonic strongholds remain secure.

Unforgiveness. This may be the greatest hindrance to deliverance. Many people have very deep wounds because of the words and actions of others. They may even believe their feelings of bitterness and resentment are justified. However, harboring unforgiveness, even in the face of the cruelest offense, is rebellion against God's command to forgive and will invite oppression (Matt. 18:34-35).

Forgiveness is the very core of Christianity. Jesus taught his disciples to pray, "Forgive us our debts, as we also have forgiven our debtors." He continued by saying:

> *For if you forgive men when they sin against you, your heavenly Father will also forgive you. But if you do not forgive men their sins, your Father will not forgive your sins. (Matt. 6:12-15)*

Some people have been hurt so deeply that they think they cannot forgive, but God would not require forgiveness if He were not ready to provide the enabling. In Matthew 18:21-35, Jesus relates a story that illustrates how small our debts to one another are in comparison to the great debt we each owed God. Meditating on this truth will help prepare a heart to forgive. Forgiveness is an act of the will in obedience to God's Word. It is not dependent upon feelings, though the feelings will follow. You might pray, "Father, in Jesus' name, I choose to forgive (name of person) and I do forgive. By faith I receive cleansing now, and renounce every spirit of unforgiveness."

It is also possible to harbor unforgiveness toward oneself. This will also hinder deliverance. In Psalm 103:12 we see that God has removed our sins as far as the east is from the west. Meditate on this and similar Scriptures. Believe that God has forgiven you. Respond to God in obedience and faith. Then when the enemy brings condemnation, resist him with the truth.

Unbelief. Unbelief will hinder you from receiving deliverance, since faith is the key to receiving anything from God. Take the time to learn what the Word of God teaches about your union with Christ, the authority you have in Him, and His desire that you be free of oppression. If a person has done this, but still is unable to believe, he may have a spirit of unbelief. He should renounce spirits of unbelief. As freedom comes, faith can then be released to continue in other areas of need.

Fear of the supernatural. This can manifest as either a distorted fear of God or a fear of Satan. Both are demonic in nature. God is a supernatural God and Christians should not fear demonstrations of His power, especially as it is demonstrated on their behalf. Understanding the great love of God as revealed in Scripture will dispel fear (1 John 4:18). Fear of Satan's power will also hinder freedom. Some are fearful of demonic manifestations that may occur during deliverance and therefore hold back from allowing deliverance to take place. These people need to be assured that God is in control and He will not allow the devil to do anything that would harm them.

Pride. Just as pride keeps multitudes out of the kingdom, pride keeps many within the kingdom from acknowledging their need and seeking help. It can be humbling to confess to deep needs and areas of bondage, but remember: "God resists the proud, but gives grace to the humble" (James 4:6, NKJV). Don't let the enemy rob you of your freedom through pride. It is not a sin to have a demon, but it is a sin to keep it!

Lack of wisdom. Effective deliverance must be based on the Word of God and applied with the wisdom of the Holy Spirit. Listen to the Holy Spirit's direction and you will avoid errors that stem from ignorance. We can ask God for wisdom with the assurance that it is His will to grant it to us:

> *If any of you lacks wisdom, he should ask God, who gives generously to all without finding fault, and it will be given to him. (Jam. 1:5)*

Lack of perseverance. Years of problems will not always be dealt with successfully in one hour of counseling and deliverance. Release from oppression may take time and continued effort. Warfare is work! Many become discouraged and give up before they experience their full freedom.

Consider the life of Joseph. Psalm 105:16-22 gives us a glimpse of Joseph's hardship. This innocent, godly young man endured years of anguish waiting for God's promise to him to be fulfilled. "Until the time that His word came to pass, the Lord tested him" (v. 19, NKJV).

In the midst of the battles, learn to focus on what God is doing, rather than on what the devil is doing. We must surrender to God's full plan and purpose for our lives while we resist the devil:

Submit yourselves, then, to God. Resist the devil, and he will flee from you. (Jam. 4:7)

The Lord is more interested in what He is making us into, than in our comfort. As we persevere in overcoming the adversary in our own lives, and as our spiritual muscles are daily strengthened, we are preparing ourselves for His eternal purposes for our lives.

DELIVERANCE FOR CHILDREN

Parents of children should realize the tremendous responsibility they have to guide and protect their children. The home environment should be one of love and security in which the children are trained in the ways of the Lord from the earliest years. Fathers must realize that a child's concept of the heavenly Father is being molded from impressions of the father in the home.

Parents should be sensitive to the needs of their children and be alert to any inroads the devil may try to make. A child may come home from school feeling rejected and inferior after being taunted by other children. The parents should comfort him and encourage him to have the right response to those who have hurt him, and pray with him. This will help keep the doors closed to demonic oppression.

Children can easily grasp the realities of spiritual conflict and should be taught to do their part in walking close to Jesus. As they learn to walk in obedience to God's Word and are encouraged to choose continually the way of righteousness, they are protected from many of the enemy's wiles.

Of course, prevention is best, but sometimes demonic oppression occurs. For example, adopted children are almost sure to need deliverance in the areas of rejection and insecurity. Other children may suffer from occult oppression through no fault of their own. In cases where deliverance is necessary for a child, it can be dealt with in sensitivity on the basis of the faith of the parent(s). A parent can come to God in faith just as the Syro-Phoenician woman obtained deliverance for her child (Mark 7:24-30).

In the case of a young child, a parent may simply rebuke spirits and pray over the child while the child sleeps. Lay your hands on the child and speak quietly against the enemy. Be positive in your words. Initially you can name the spirits you are commanding, but then emphasize the positive. For example in dealing with a spirit of rebellion, you might say, "Spirits of rebellion, we command you in the name of Jesus to go out. We loose this child by the power of the blood of Jesus. We set his mind and will free from these pressures. Every band is broken in the name of Jesus. There is no more place for you here." Follow up with the affirmations from the Word of love and victory for your child.

If you pray while the child is awake, it should be done with his or her cooperation. Be sure the child is not overly tired or active, though some spirits can cause agitation or sleepiness to distract you and stop you from forcing them out. Use language that will not instill fear in the child. Instead of saying "evil spirit," you might say, "we come against this hold of rejection in Jesus' name." Quote Scriptures that apply to the area of need.

It may be best to minister to the child daily or weekly for a period of time to see him through to full freedom. Deliverance will be maintained as the child is trained in God's ways under the protective prayers of the parent(s).

GROUP DELIVERANCE

It is possible that an entire church or group within the church may have a common need for deliverance in a specific area. In such a case, a leader may determine that group deliverance is expedient, rather than a series of individual sessions.

Deliverance may be initiated at the discretion of the leadership after the subject is dealt with in a teaching and the group is adequately instructed and prepared to fight the enemy. The leader should guide the group through deliverance, naming the spirits and commanding them out, as the group looks to the Lord in faith, believing that the power of the cross has set them free. It is important for the leader to maintain order, not allowing fleshly demonstrations, indiscreet behavior, or demonic control of the session (1 Cor. 14:40). Trained helpers may stand by ready to minister to those experiencing difficulty in getting set free.

DELIVERANCE OF HOMES AND BUILDINGS

Spirits can linger in homes or buildings. The legal ground for their presence can be present or past sin, or objects that have spirits attached or associated with them. These may include a statue with religious significance brought in from another country or even many popular children's toys.

Cleansing your home or place of business is not difficult. Walk through the building, praying and dedicating the home or property to the Lord, believing that the Holy Spirit will show you what you need to know. Any occult objects should be removed and destroyed (Acts 19:19). Ask God to cleanse the sins that allowed entrance to demons and put these under the blood of Jesus. Cast out the evil spirits in the name of Jesus, then declare the place set apart to God through the power of the blood of Jesus Christ. This can be done from room to room taking time to discern any hindrances or specific names of spirits.

STUDY QUESTIONS

1. Why must a Christian involved in deliverance ministry be part of a local church?
2. Explain the importance of forgiveness in deliverance ministry.
3. Describe three manifestations Jesus encountered as He drove out demons.
4. Name three hindrances to deliverance and explain how to overcome them.

Conclusion

The Scriptures show that evil will increase until the coming of the Lord Jesus. As we draw closer to the end, we can expect to see the tragic effects of demonic oppression on every hand.

In the midst of this darkness, the church is called to rise up with the authority that God has given us in Jesus Christ, and through the power of the Holy Spirit to continue the work of Jesus Christ as His representatives on earth.

> *...For this purpose the Son of God was manifested, that He might destroy the works of the devil. (1 John 3:8, NKJV)*

Selected Bibliography

Anderson, Neil T. *The Bondage Breaker.* Eugene, Oregon: Harvest House Publishers. 1990.

Davis, John J. *Demons, Exorcism and the Evangelical.* Winona Lake, Indiana: BMH Books. 1977.

Freeman, Hobart. *Angels of Light?* Plainfield, New Jersey: Logos International. 1969.

Hammond, Frank and Ida Mae. *Pigs in the Parlor.* Kirkwood, Missouri: Impact Books. 1973.

MacMillan, John A. *Encounter With Darkness.* Harrisburg, Pennsylvania: Christian Publications. 1980.

Miller, Glen and Erma. *Some Things We Have Learned About Deliverance.* Hot Springs, Arkansas: Lake Hamilton Bible Camp. 1988.

Powell, Graham and Shirley. *Christian Set Yourself Free.* Kent, England: Sovereign World Ltd. 1983.

Prosser, Peter E. *Knowing How To Operate in Signs and Wonders.* Virginia Beach, Virginia: Regent University. 1994.

Smith, Eddie & Alice. *Intercessors & Pastors: The Emerging Partnership of Watchmen & Gatekeepers.* Houston, TX: SpiriTruth Publishing. 2000.

Smith, Eddie. *A Chain, a Key, and a Command: The Believer's Authority to Wrestle Against Principalities.* Houston, TX. 1997.

Unger, Merrill F. *Biblical Demonology.* Wheaton, Illinois: Van Kampen Press. 1952.

Unger, Merrill F. *Demons in the World Today.* Wheaton, Illinois: Tyndale House Pub. 1971.

Webber, Malcolm. *The Blood of God.* Goshen, IN: Pioneer Books. 1992.

Whyte, H.A. Maxwell. *Demons and Deliverance.* Springdale, Pennsylvania: Whitaker House. 1989.

Wimber, John and Kevin Springer. *Power Healing.* New York: Harper and Row. 1987.

Strategic Press
www.StrategicPress.org

Strategic Press is a division of Strategic Global Assistance, Inc.
www.sgai.org

513 S. Main St. Suite 2
Elkhart, IN 46516
U.S.A

+1-844-532-3371 (LEADER-1)

www.ingramcontent.com/pod-product-compliance
Lightning Source LLC
Chambersburg PA
CBHW072158100426
42738CB00011BA/2466